A **MATTER** of **RECOVERY**

The Story of C.B. Miller

C.B. Miller (signature)

Thank you! (handwritten)

WES SKILLINGS

Wes S. (signature)

LifeRich PUBLISHING®

LifeRich Publishing is a registered trademark of
The Reader's Digest Association, Inc.

LifeRich Publishing books may be ordered through booksellers or by contacting:

LifeRich Publishing
1663 Liberty Drive
Bloomington, IN 47403
www.liferichpublishing.com
1 (888) 238-8637

Because of the dynamic nature of the Internet, any web addresses or
links contained in this book may have changed since publication and
may no longer be valid. The views expressed in this work are solely those
of the author and do not necessarily reflect the views of the publisher,
and the publisher hereby disclaims any responsibility for them.

Any people depicted in stock imagery provided by Thinkstock are models,
and such images are being used for illustrative purposes only.
Certain stock imagery © Thinkstock.

ISBN: 978-1-4897-0301-9 (sc)
ISBN: 978-1-4897-0300-2 (hc)
ISBN: 978-1-4897-0302-6 (e)

Library of Congress Control Number: 2014915773

Printed in the United States of America.

LifeRich Publishing rev. date: 10/30/2014

A MATTER OF RECOVERY

For C. B. Miller

What makes you good at your game,
And helps you to come out ahead?
"Discipline and concentration,
And hard work," the team coach said.

"You do what you have to do
And stay until the job is done:
Nothing can be finished
Unless, first, it is begun."

I asked coach to tell me
Where his confidence was bred
And how I could find it
If I followed where he led.
"Discipline and concentration.
You work at it," he said,
"And you do what you do
Without fear of what's ahead!"

-Alfred S. Groh
10/18/94

To C.B.
Coach DeMelfi
Alfred S. Groh

FOREWORD

I will never forget the phone call we received from C.B.'s sister, Maurie, telling us that he was in the hospital fighting for his life after falling three stories off a balcony at a friend's apartment in Wilkes Barre, PA. The news was mind numbing, like being doused with ice water after taking a steaming hot bath. As my wife, Bronwyn, and I later drove from our home near Boston to the Wilkes Barre General Hospital, we were extremely concerned and full of questions. How was C. B.? How serious were his injuries? Was he going to survive?

We had known C. B. since the day he was born. He was the youngest of Mike and Sharon Miller's four children, all of them great young people. His father and I had been friends since early childhood and had gone to school together. We had watched C. B. grow into a big, strong, smart, and quick-witted young man who loved sports, played them with considerable skill, and ended up at Wilkes College on the varsity football team. As a historian, I was especially pleased when he told me one day that he was thinking about becoming a history teacher and coaching at the high school level. His future looked bright. Then came the fall that changed his life.

When Bronwyn and I arrived at the hospital, we didn't know what to expect. It soon became apparent that C. B. was in serious trouble. In an induced coma, he was in the intensive care unit with a cervical collar, eyes that looked like purple golf balls, and what appeared to be life-support tubes connected to virtually every part of his body. While his parents and three siblings put up a good front, it was clear from the pained look in their eyes and drawn faces that the situation was dire. They were understandably shell-shocked, trying to understand the medical options being presented to them, the tenuous/uncertain state of C. B.'s condition, and the pressing need to make decisions as to what should be done next. Thank God their oldest son, Mike Jr., was there. He had recently graduated from medical school, knew the procedures being employed, and briefed his parents continuously on the state of C.B.'s condition, translating seemingly incomprehensible medical jargon into laymen's language and helping his parents make informed decisions about what (or what not) to do next. It must have been particularly difficult for him to be a detached doctor and a caring brother at the same time!

When we left Wilkes-Barre that day, we still didn't know what to think. We knew that C. B. was in extremely serious condition and that things were "touch and go," especially persistent concerns about the swelling of his brain. On the other hand, we found it difficult to believe that a big, strong guy like C.B. was going to die. To be sure, we knew it was a possibility, but somehow we felt he was going to pull through. Like everyone around him, we thought of him constantly and prayed for his recovery. Only much later did we learn that the fall had destroyed half of C.B.'s brain and that his recovery, if ever, was going to be a long, difficult process. But recover he did, and in the process, he not only retained his outgoing personality, wit, and charm, he also recaptured his intellect and, with it, gained a lot of wisdom. It was as if he had grown up all over again.

C. B.'s parents, Mike and Sharon, frequently refer to his recovery as "a miracle," and we agree. The story of C. B.'s comeback, so skillfully told by Wes Skillings, speaks volumes not only about C.B.'s strength of character and determination to recover but also the caring tenacity/stick-to-itiveness of his family and friends. In addition to telling the remarkable story of C. B. and his voyage of rediscovery, the following pages provide an instructive primer on the nature of brain injuries, their many twists and turns, and complex implications. Families with brain-injured loved ones will find this book extremely helpful in negotiating the complex and often frustrating turns a person's recovery takes, helping them to think out appropriate strategies, decisions, and therapies for the recovery process. Indeed, what I like best about this book is that it tells several stories and integrates them extremely well: the story of C. B. and his rediscovery process; the story of brain injuries, what they entail, and how one deals/copes with them at multiple levels of experience; and, perhaps most important of all, the story of how family and friends provided C. B. the love and support he needed to make the long journey to rehabilitation and rediscovery.

We knew C. B. had turned the corner when he and his parents came to visit at our summer place in Maine some months after his fall. His mobility and speech were still hesitant, but one could see that he was striving to make progress. There was a beer commercial on TV at that time showing frogs croaking out the syllables of "Bud-wei-ser." C. B. would mimic the ad with a big grin on his face. At one point I happened to use the word "ambiance" in describing some now forgotten place. C. B.'s ears perked up and he asked about the word. After hearing the word again, he grinned and immediately began reciting it in drawn-out syllables, "am-bi-ance," like the commercial. We all laughed, and "Am-Bi-Ance" became the catchword for the rest of the visit and well beyond. All anyone had to do was just start the "Am" and the rest of us would chime in with the other syllables. To us, "ambiance" will always be linked with the amazing story of C. B. Miller's comeback, and the faith, love, and determination that made it happen.

Merritt Roe Smith
Cutten Professor of the History of Technology
STS and History Faculties
Massachusetts Institute of Technology

PREFACE

Twenty years ago, my life took a dramatic turn when my son, C.B., fell from a third-story balcony and sustained a traumatic brain injury. At first, I wanted only that my son survive. As it turned out, survival was just the beginning of a very long journey, one that continues even today.

My wife, Sharon, and I believe we have witnessed a miracle. The chances of our son's survival were slim, yet he defied the odds. What's more, the progress C.B. has made throughout his recovery is nothing short of phenomenal. We are so profoundly grateful for the second chance we've been given with our son, and to all of those who helped us along the way, including those who've helped us write this book.

When we decided to find a way to share C.B.'s story with a larger audience, we realized we needed help. We turned to our friend Wes Skillings, who had retired in 2011 from his long time position of editor at a local weekly newspaper. Throughout a career that spanned four decades, Wes had been a reporter, editor and columnist. His work has been recognized by the Pennsylvania Newspaper Association, which awarded Wes 15 Keystone Press Awards between 1997 and 2011. Wes first met C.B. when he wrote a feature article about his recovery. When we asked if he might be willing and able to help us write this book, he graciously agreed.

Wes spent endless hours researching, interviewing, and retracing the steps of C.B. and our family from the unfortunate accident, through acute rehabilitation, and ultimately to where C.B. is today. "This is more than a story about a unique person who came back from a devastating injury," Wes says. "It is a primer that could open doors of possibilities for others with TBI and those who love them."

Once Wes had written the book, our daughter, Kathie, spent some time editing it. Who knew that the daughter we thought might be speech impaired as a toddler would grow up to have such a way with words. We are thankful to her for lending us her gift to help us get this book ready for publication.

As we worked on the book, we kept trying to come up with a title. Sharon eventually found inspiration for what we think is the perfect fit. The title for this book "A Matter of Recovery: The Story of C. B. Miller" was taken from a poem written for C. B. by the late Alfred

S. Groh. Alfred was the husband of Jane Lampe Groh who was the Dean of Student Affairs at Wilkes University at the time of C.B.'s accident. Jane was one of the first ones to meet us when we arrived at the hospital. She emerged from a group of C.B.'s friends, introduced herself and quickly became an invaluable resource as well as a source of incredible strength. She, Al and their family became very dear friends and a critical source of support for us over the years.

For all those named in this preface, as well as the many additional names you will read in the following pages, there are countless others who've contributed to our efforts. We thank each and every one of them. We could not have done this without their love and support.

Mike Miller

CHAPTER 1

DISAPPEARING INTO THE DARKNESS

Blueberries.

Sharon Miller still vividly remembers the scene as she and her husband, Mike, drove away from dropping off their son, C.B., at the apartment he shared with friend and fellow Wilkes University student, Jack Swearhart.

Jack and C.B. were casually tossing blueberries into their mouths on this warm summer afternoon in Wilkes-Barre, PA. It was about 1:30 p.m., and Sharon's fleeting image of her son was the last she'd see him as he used to be.

It was just another summer's day, even forgettable had it not been seared into their memories later. C.B. Miller was excited about the prospect of playing football as a collegian, and summer practices were coming soon. The imposing 275-pound junior, rallying from an earlier injury, had been undergoing rigorous conditioning for months to play on the line for the Wilkes Colonels. On this particular day,

1

July 21, 1994, a Thursday, Mike and Sharon Miller had used some vacation time to spend a few days with their eldest son, Michael, Jr., who was interning at Crozer Chester Hospital in the Philadelphia suburb of Chester. C.B. had gone with them, but he had to get back to his summer job at the Woodlands Inn, a popular resort on the threshold of the Poconos, that evening.

His brother, Mike, would remember leaving his apartment early for work that morning. There were hugs and kisses for his parents, but C.B. was still in bed and he had stirred just enough to extend a hand from underneath the covers.

"I never really saw his face," Mike recalls. "Looking back, it was the last time I shook his right hand when it was still vital and strong." Shaking your brother's hand can be a big deal when you think of it that way.

The Millers left later that morning, with only a handful of stops between Philadelphia and Wilkes-Barre, linked by the Northeast Extension of the Pennsylvania Turnpike. They would drop C.B. off there at Jack's apartment over a storefront just a couple of blocks off the city's Public Square. He would be staying there until he moved into a dorm when the fall semester began. His parents would continue another sixty-five miles to the north and obliquely west to their home in Towanda, like Wilkes-Barre situated on the North Branch of the Susquehanna River. C.B. would go to his job that afternoon — something subsequently erased from his memory—and, later that evening, after busing tables on the dinner shift, he decided to check out a gathering at the third-floor apartment of another college friend a short walk from his apartment.

C.B. had been there before, but he doesn't remember being there on the evening of July 21, 1994. He certainly doesn't remember walking out on the balcony or leaning on that railing. That rotten railing.

Funny the things you remember. They had purchased laundry detergent for C.B. and Sharon realized, upon arriving home, that the soap was still in the car. As it turned out, that soap would have been of no use to C.B. Maybe that's why the memory of that forgotten container stays with her.

Their daughter, Kathie, soon to be pursuing a graduate degree at American University in Washington, D.C., was still at home, working a summer job. She had gone to bed for the evening. All four Miller siblings were smart, but the two best students were Kathie and Michael. Kathie was the brain and Michael was the focused overachiever, who still, as he likes to say, "starts each day with a lean." That left sister, Maurita, known as Maurie, and C.B. Maurie, excelling at mathematics, holds a degree in accounting. She was working and living across the New York State border in nearby Elmira. Maurie was, and still is, good at taking care of others, setting her own ego aside. There was a close bond between Maurie and C.B., and, ever the clown, he found in her his most appreciative audience.

C.B. was definitely the underachiever when it came to school, but the hulking 21-year-old sparkled at sports, particularly baseball, swimming and football. He loved life, people and having a good time.

He was smart enough, but he had yet to be convinced of the merits of scholarly pursuits. There was about a two-year gap between each of the Miller kids, starting with Michael, followed by Maurie, Kathie and C.B. Michael loved sports, playing backup quarterback in football and achieving more distinction as a starting catcher on his high school baseball team, the Towanda Black Knights. Maurie, the math whiz, loved to get involved in school fundraisers. Kathie was the academic who excelled in school but was also involved in a lot of extracurricular activities, including cheerleading and student council.

Then there was C.B. His given name is Christopher Bradley Miller, but by that time he was known to just about everyone by his initials. That he walks among us today, hobbled and physically altered from his injuries, is, in the minds of many, a miracle. It is a miracle, some would argue, that he survived the accident that sent him plummeting some three stories head-first into an alley below on a summer's eve, destroying 40 percent of his brain. Eradicated within milliseconds upon impact was virtually the left front, a repository for, among other functions, problem solving, behavior, personality, emotions, speech, understanding and control of the right side of his body. There was also rampant devastation to the parts of the brain affecting reading, writing, spatial relationships, sensation, perception and memory.

They would discover, through pain and suffering, how truly amazing the human brain is in bridging the gap from massive destruction of brain cells to working cells that may seem to have nothing to do with the functions that have been lost. His brother, the doctor, describes it as "cross talk," pointing out that you can take out half the brain of a child and still retain most, if not all, the functions of the other side. Autopsies, going back as far as 130 years, have revealed people who have enjoyed productive, gratifying lives after having as much as half of their brains destroyed.

He knows that today, but back in the summer of 1994 the young intern understood the components of traumatic brain injury—the fundamentals of treating for survival— but acknowledges that he still didn't understand the chronic implications, what C.B. would be facing should he survive.

There is brain, but there is also heart and soul. Some seem to have more of the latter than others, and C.B. Miller, blessed by youth and a competitive spirit, would prove he had plenty to spare. As is often the case with Traumatic Brain Injury (TBI) survivors, science and medicine are inadequate to explain why things turn out the way they do. July 21, 1994, would trigger the beginning of his new life, and there would be no football ever again for the burly collegian. A dilapidated balcony railing outside a friend's apartment changed all of that.

"I was talking, not thinking, and I leaned on it," he recalls. Actually, there is no recollection in his severely damaged brain—either of the fall itself or the handful of hours preceding it. What he knows about that evening comes from the others who were there, other Wilkes students, who had no time to react when the railing snapped away and all 275 pounds of the old C.B. Miller were gone just like that. It was in the vicinity of 10:30 in the evening in the City of Wilkes-Barre, and some speculate that the hurtling C.B. instinctively tried to grab for something, anything, on an adjacent building just a few feet from the edge of the balcony. In fact, he may have literally caromed off the other building before dashing the left side of his skull into the unforgiving hardness below. C.B. was later told that the distance between the balcony and where he landed was forty-two feet, and he remains fascinated by the number "42." Imagine the impact of such a large man, barely 21 years old, falling that far head-first. A severely injured left arm may have broken the fall just slightly. Then again, slightly may have saved his life.

Maybe that was the difference between living and dying. More likely it was a fellow student and a former combat soldier with medical training, Stefan Clausen, who, seconds after the fall, was able to turn C.B.'s fractured and bleeding head slightly, clearing his airway, maintaining the flow of life-saving oxygen to the brain. It may have been because he was only minutes away via ambulance to Wilkes-Barre General Hospital, where numerous surgeries, each critical in its own right, would extend the miracle over the ensuing weeks. There would be at least fourteen different specialists involved in both saving his life and subsequent recovery.

And then there was his physical condition, thanks to working out for the impending football season. There was no alcohol in his system, the presence of which may have wrought further complications. He was drinking water that night at the casual gathering of friends.

"When I think about that night, I'm thinking that the one guy who wasn't drinking is the guy who gets hurt," says Clausen who launched a start-up technology company after leaving a management position at a globally recognized information and research organization.

"He leaned back… and he was gone"

The keg was out on the balcony of what Clausen remembers as "this cruddy apartment" and a number of them had spilled out there, content to breathe in the summer night air and stay close to the beer. Clausen was about to embark on his senior year at Wilkes, and was three or four years older than most of the other students there. He had been out in the world, learning some hard facts of life as an Army grunt and paratrooper. He had seen some serious stuff and had hand's-on training pertaining to injuries a combat soldier might encounter during the time of Operations Desert Storm and Desert Shield. For instance, he knew how to treat a sucking chest wound and basic responses to traumatic injuries.

It is very likely C.B. Miller would have died had not Stefan Clausen been in the mood for some company and a few beers. Clausen still remembers the events of that night almost eighteen years before with great clarity.

"I was talking to him when it happened. He leaned back against the railing and he was gone. Just like that. He was there one moment and then he disappeared into the darkness."

Momentarily stunned, but only momentarily, the adrenalin-charged Clausen fled the apartment down the front stairs, with another student, Reggie Stencil, following. They emerged between two storefronts, U-turning into the alley where, at the far end of the building, they found C.B. lying on his back with what was unmistakably a massive head trauma. Quickly surveying the dimly lit scene, Clausen saw that C.B.'s head had apparently struck the rounded bar of a metal railing next to a pair of steps leading up out of the back of the alley into a parking lot. The big man had toppled over on his back. It was bone into metal. He still remembers the scene vividly.

The first thing Clausen did was lie down next to C.B.

"I sort of aligned my body with his, to stabilize his neck and spine. His throat was filled with blood, and I'm thinking he's gotta breathe." That's when, pressed against the much larger man, he slowly, gently turned his head to the side to clear his airway, letting the pooled blood run out and the air in.

C.B. was born and raised in Towanda, the county seat of rural Bradford County, where he most likely would have been in the summer between semesters had he not been employed busing tables at the Woodlands just outside Wilkes-Barre. Had such a devastating accident occurred in Towanda, valuable time would have been consumed in an ambulance ride and then airlifting him to a regional facility equipped to deal with traumatic brain injury.

"His best chance of survival came from falling where he was, short of falling directly into the E.R.," says his brother, now a doctor and vascular interventional radiology specialist at Duke University School of Medicine in Durham, N.C. Michael was a recent medical school graduate and interning in Philadelphia—in a hospital emergency room no less— when he got the late-night call about C.B.'s fall.

He would play a valuable role as an intermediary between his family and the medical staff at Wilkes-Barre General during the most critical hours, even to the point of having a neurosurgeon replaced who had adopted a wait-and-see attitude as his brother hovered close to death.

Michael Miller, Jr., M.D. is a pragmatist who, despite his Catholic upbringing, is hesitant about proclaiming miracles. It is more about statistics, beating some huge odds. He feels that if his brother had taken that plunge 100 times, he may have survived six times, at most, and maybe just once or twice in those six nonfatal falls he might have gone on to live anything approaching a normal life.

Nobody would have predicted then that C.B. Miller would go on to earn a college degree, though it would be a painstaking process requiring special tutoring, even literacy training, and revisiting classes at his old high school. Finally, there would be the deliberate process of earning college credits one course at a time over a span of eleven years. He gives motivational talks on a regular basis to various audiences ranging from at-risk kids to college-level physical therapy and special education students at the University of Scranton and Mansfield University, respectively. He walks with a noticeable limp and has virtually no use of his right arm. All of the corrective surgeries can't hide the damage to the left side of his head, particularly a left eye that was once literally separated from its smashed eye socket. He has cried no tears from that eye at least, because he has to manually lubricate it with drops.

"What can I say?" he says when asked if he is at all self-conscious about the physical reminders of his massive injuries. "I'm a very sexy man."

That's the most amazing thing about C.B. Miller. He is a funny, and genuinely sociable, person. If he harbors any bitterness about his fate, he has assuredly gotten over it. There was a time, he confesses, when he was mad at God for letting it be him, but then he thinks it may be more about a higher calling. Even though he was closing in on the age of forty, middle age, in 2012, he feels he was essentially reborn on July 21, 1994. By that reckoning, he would be turning eighteen on his next birthday.

"That was the day I got a new brother," is the blunt assessment of his sibling, the doctor. So much of the old C.B. remains intact, including his dry and self-deprecating sense of humor, but he will not be the high school history teacher he had planned to be nor will sports—once so important in his life—be anything more to him than something to watch, sparking fond memories of his own athletic prowess. Yet he is still a popular and well-known figure in his hometown, where he lives independently in his own apartment with intervention from his parents that decreased over time.

He'll walk right up to people and engage them in a conversation, ask a question or crack a joke. He gets in your space, and that can be intimidating for some who don't know him. Yet most come to like him in a matter of minutes and, if they don't, C.B. doesn't take it personally.

There are only two things that bother C.B. as far as the attitudes of other people. Some, he says, think he is faking it because he is essentially living on disability and funds made possible by the awarding of civil damages as a result of his accident.

"Why would I want to fake being disabled?" he asks incredulously. "It took a lot of hard work getting back to where I am. I can't read or write really, but I got a college degree the hard way and taking it one step at a time. It's why I keep getting better, a little at a time, even after all of these years."

"C.B. has a lot of perseverance and a lot of drive. He's not going to sit around and do nothing," Maurie says. "He could easily do that, and he could have easily just sat around and not gone to college and lived life and done whatever he wanted to do. Instead, he chose to defy all odds and push himself."

He doesn't understand why, though the details of his accident should be familiar to those in his small town, there are still those who say he was drinking when he fell off that balcony. It's as if these people are saying he somehow deserved what happened to him, and C.B. is mystified why this storyline fails to go away. It's not that drugs and alcohol were foreign to C.B. His previous attempt at college, a disastrous freshman outing several years before his accident, attest to that. He got into partying and cutting classes, focusing more on baseball than academics.

"I didn't really need drinking to be funny or popular, but I guess it just made it easier to have a good time," he explains between sporadic pauses, the remnants of his aphasia. The limp, as he throws his damaged right leg stiffly and jauntily ahead when he walks, and that uncooperative right arm, are the immediate physical signs you notice. Then as you pick up some face time, there's the bloodshot left eye that seems to look over the top of you and a head that isn't quite symmetrical.

Coming back: a work in progress

Only the aphasia betrays that something isn't quite right inside. Sometimes things don't connect as he talks—a word that needs to be searched for or losing a train of thought. C.B. is never stymied, though. He always comes up with something and the conversation continues with those fits and starts. Fascinatingly, his speech pattern is not so different from high-IQ, professorial types whose brains race ahead of their speech, reining back from time to time, creating a halting speech pattern.

Here is a man who was in a coma for more than five weeks, some of it drug-induced to allow his battered brain to heal. He could not talk for months, including most of the way through four months of in-patient physical therapy at the John Heinz Institute of Rehabilitation Medicine on the outskirts of Wilkes-Barre. It was a breakthrough to hear him say "yes" and "no," his basic vocabulary for too long. C.B.

remembers the frustration of the words being in there and not being able to get them out. That's pretty much what aphasia is, but back then it was as if the words were locked inside his crumpled brain and the key, if there was one, couldn't be found.

It's been some twenty years, and he is still healing, still getting better. It is true he has his good and bad days, and when he gets tired the aphasia is more pronounced. An afternoon nap became part of his routine, and when his battery is recharged he can keep up with anyone in a conversation. Let down your guard, and he'll get the best of you, but he likes nothing better than a quip at his own expense. In the summer of 2012, he decided to forego his nap—still another step in a recovery process with ongoing goals.

C.B. Miller is dedicated to making a contribution to the world around him, whether through motivational speaking or the photographs he shoots and sells. He is a natural in front of groups, the bigger the better, and he has the timing of a stand-up comic, playing off people in his audiences and mostly making fun of himself. He is never mean-spirited, but likes to tease people behind a serious countenance that elicits its share of double-takes. His unique laugh— somewhere between a cackle and giggle— is seldom far behind.

Phil Gianficaro, a sports columnist for the Citizen's Voice in Wilkes-Barre at the time, speculated months after the accident that C.B. stood for "Coming Back." That was at a time when he was barely communicative and wheelchair bound, embarking on the rehab journey to relearn how to walk and talk. If only Gianficaro, now writing for the Intelligencer in Newtown, PA, and Bucks County Times, could see him now.

The story of C.B. Miller's coming back is a work in progress, as it has been since the ambulance first delivered him to the emergency room of Wilkes-Barre General Hospital late on the evening of July 21, 1994. The focus was, at first, saving his life. From there it was re-establishing some quality to his life. And now it has become what C.B. can do to bring something of meaning to the lives of others.

None of it could have been done without some outstanding people, but none are more so than the family that has been there for him all along. His parents, Mike and Sharon Miller, now both in their seventies, have done all they can to make C.B. not only independent but proactive as they have been and as they have taught their children to be.

Craig Dawsey is a high school football coach and teacher in Towanda who regularly brings C.B. in to speak to his eighth graders. When he is asked to describe Mike Miller and his efforts on behalf of his youngest son, one word comes to his mind: "Relentless."

Although this is C.B. Miller's story, often viewed from his perspective, this is also about a family and a father who recognized quickly the value of being proactive and how critical it is to be your own advocate.

"We quit thinking a long time ago in the terms of rehabilitation and started thinking of it in terms of rediscovery," Mike Miller says today.

Welcome to C.B. Miller's journey of rediscovery and the mysteries of the human brain.

CHAPTER 2

BUILDING BRIDGES IN THE BRAIN

We've all heard it before: "Most of us use no more than ten percent of our brainpower." This generally held truism is perhaps exaggeration, speculation, or even myth. What seems to be the actual case is that we don't fully understand the powers and functionality of the brain. A complex organ, the brain is comprised of many parts, each with varied functions. Only with advancements in sophisticated imaging techniques have we been able to measure and better understand the brain, how it works, and how we use it.

C.B. Miller lost forty percent of his brain function, yet he's able to get by and leads an independent life. What's more, he still possesses the sharp wit for which he was known even before the fall. He's able to joke, jest, and make just about anyone laugh. C.B. might not always remember names and words, but he can express himself in ways that clearly convey he has a keen sense of humor.

Lessons in comedy are not part of rehabilitation or therapy for the brain injured. C.B. did not relearn his sense of humor. It just seemed to be there, even able to resurface before therapy helped him regain use of expressive language, literal reasoning, verbal memory, and sequencing the components of a story. Therapy may have helped him more effectively express his sense of humor, but he reconnected with his inner comedian all on his own. And this was key to his recovery.

There is no scientific explanation for what constitutes humor, particularly its deficiencies and excesses. One person's humor is another's irritant. C.B. was something of a class clown whose humor wasn't always appreciated. His mother, Sharon, remembers going to the high school for parent-teacher conferences. "We'd go into one and the teacher would say, 'Oh, he's got such a fantastic sense of humor. He adds so much to the class." The next one: 'I'm pulling my hair out. This kid is too much of the clown and he's disturbing the class.'"

Yet, she remembers the elation she felt when she realized his sense of humor was intact. He was still at Heinz, the rehab center, but home for the weekend about a week before the Christmas of 1994, when a visiting family friend was commenting about his wife frequently complaining that he talked too loud. With exquisite timing, C.B. cupped his hand to his ear and said, "What?" Even when he was barely more than monosyllabic, he could turn it into humor. It was music that tended to open him up. Whatever the source of humor may be, singing and speaking are known to come from different parts of the brain. C.B., of course, would bring all three together.

Sister, Kathie, was sitting on the couch when he made his first trip home from the rehab center for Thanksgiving four months after the fall. It was afternoon. The digital clock said 3:33, and remembering the doctors' advice to work with him on regaining basic skills, she asked him what time it was. She felt the repetition of the same number might make it easier for him.

"He looks at me. He looks at the clock. He looks back at me and then I could see him try and then an expression came over his face that was like, 'Uh, oh, get ready for it,' because I knew that something was about to happen. Then he started to sing. It was like, 'Once, Twice, Three Times a Lady' without any effort. He couldn't say 3-3-3. He knew the number and was trying to get at it, and that's how he did it. You could see this twinkle in is eye as he came up with the solution."

"He throws back his head and laughs, a real belly laugh, and he had that from the beginning," says Sylvia Abrams, a middle school reading teacher who started working with C.B. when he had a total vocabulary of no more than 50 words. "Plays on words and little jokes and always the wholehearted laugh. He had that strong sense of humor from the beginning."

"I'm a sexy man," he likes to say, gauging your reaction. He worked at a nightclub and resort, The Woodlands Inn, the summer of his accident, which included multiple bars and entertainment by DJs and bands at night. "I was a strip teaser there," he says deadpan. "The girls would be yelling, 'Put it back on! Put it back on!' I got a couple of quarters out of it."

The humor is almost always aimed at himself. If he trusts you, regards you as a friend, then he'll include you as a target of his humor.

The brain builds bridges between the hemispheres of its cerebral cortex. It's the "cross talk" referenced by C.B.'s brother, the physician and man of science. Destroyed brain cells don't come back to life—even the ones we lose via the aging process— but others mysteriously take over lost functions. Recovery from TBI is enhanced by youth. C.B. was young, not much more than a kid at the age of 21, and his brain had something going for it—plasticity. The more you have of that, the better the brain can compensate, adapting to injury and other invaders, internal and external. The bridge crew must have been working overtime to rebuild and reconnect through that extended coma and those frustrating weeks when the words wouldn't come out, and, when they did, it was a word here and there, usually yes or no.

How a sense of humor, or any of our unique personality traits, survive such devastating damage to the frontal lobe, for example, may never be adequately explained. There is only one certainty about brain injury: no two of them are alike. There was nobody exactly like C.B. Miller before his accident, and the same is true of the C.B. Miller who has emerged since the accident.

Defying logic with a lot of soul...

Then there is what his brother calls his "crumple zone." C.B. used up all of his. His face and skull collapsed when they met with metal and hard earth that summer night. The face and skull are intended to serve as protection for the brain. With this "crumple zone" compromised upon impact, much of C.B.'s brain was compromised with it. What remained was a complex mixture and, as it turns out, magical and otherworldly. Make that innerworldly. Otherworldy, after all, simply means something that is not of this world. The brain creates its own world. It can take you away, separate you from the commonplace, and sometimes collide with logic.

The treatment of brain injury has come a long way since July of 1994. In recent years, there have been some famous people who have been felled by traumatic brain injury. C.B. Miller is just one of more than five million survivors of TBI, according to the National Institute of Neurological Disorders and Stroke. They live with a permanent TBI-related disability, and though most garner little attention, there have been some famous survivors in recent years. The ongoing recovery of Congresswoman Gabrielle "Gabby" Giffords captured the country's attention. Her comeback, too, has been miraculous—almost as amazing as her bringing the warring Democrats and Republicans together, if only briefly, in the celebration of her return to the House Chamber. That makes brain injury one of the few causes in recent memory that is nonpartisan— at least for an hour or two.

Perhaps such a comeback is a reaffirmation that the soul, not the brain, is what really rules. It's not all measurable. It defies logic and therefore makes all things possible. It is also why the brain and the mind are not really the same thing. Cognition is a function of the brain —putting things together and solving problems through reasoning, thinking and logic. But most of us would define what's at play in such a comeback as relating more to the soul and the mind, because the process seems too subtle and complex to be relegated to a mass of convoluted tissue.

Reductionism seems to prevail in the study of the brain, breaking the whole down into the functions of its separate parts. You can weigh, study and dissect the brain, but where do you begin dissecting the mind, which some cultures believe to be the seat of the soul? Reducing anything to its most elemental parts, a great pitcher's fastball to movement and reactions of muscles and tendons in the shoulder and arm, for instance, is like explaining Einstein's genius by electrical impulses, neurotransmitters, brain waves and synapses.

"I maintain that the human mystery is incredibly demeaned by scientific reductionism," stated John Eccles, Nobel Prize winning neurophysiologist.

Before Giffords, there was Bob Woodruff, injured by a roadside bomb while reporting on the war in Iraq back in 2006. His comeback from TBI was truly a full one, with him back on the beat as a journalist and as a vocal advocate for people with serious brain injuries. Even though Giffords' and Woodruff's stories are similar in many ways, including the surgeries and the rehab, why some people come back and others don't remain a mystery.

Courage, determination and faith all play a role, but are Giffords, Woodruff and C.B. Miller more heroic because of how far they have come than those who are totally dependent upon others for their existence? Crushed and shattered skulls requiring surgeries notwithstanding, the damage may not always be visible, turning something seemingly innocuous into something ominous.

Not much more than an hour's drive from where C.B. fell and a dozen years later, a fourteen-year-old girl bumped her head on the seat in front of her in a minor school bus collision. There was virtually no damage to the two vehicles involved and no other injuries among the other child passengers. Yet it shattered her memory and led to years of learning and behavioral disorders for what was believed initially to be a concussion, later to be diagnosed as mild TBI. It literally revamped her personality and changed the course of her future.

It opened up a Pandora's Box of darkness and doubt, as the girl essentially became learning disabled overnight, with little more than a pounding headache the morning after as a symptom of the damage incurred. Her mother, Naomi Parker, who authored a book about her daughter's journey, When Libby Lost Her Smile, explains the frustrations of suffering an injury nobody can see in a letter to a judge who presided over a civil suit on her daughter's behalf:

"Her teachers always start out supportive and understanding, but when faced with the reality of what Libby goes through, by Christmas we are at the school again fighting for her rights and trying to help teachers understand that just because they have lost patience …doesn't make this injury go away."

There was no visible injury to Parker's daughter, no facial scarring or other visual cue that might serve as a reminder to teachers, counselors and others that she required special treatment, even rehabilitation. It was literally all in her head. Now a young woman, her healing process was agonizingly slow, taking months for the smallest of gains. The remainder of her schooling became so confrontational that Parker did not use her daughter's real name in the book, though she now accompanies her at book signings.

Labeling something as mild TBI or a concussion may be a big reason why such injuries are discounted or not taken as seriously as they should be. Saying something is traumatic gets your attention. Calling something mild doesn't. This may be why it took so long for organized sports, from high school to professional, to stop treating concussions as injuries you could play through or walk off like a wrenched knee. Calling them concussions, head injuries or disorders of consciousness doesn't change what is occurring here—a brain pathology resulting from a blow or jolt from an external force.

"Isn't mild trauma an oxymoron?" asks Susan H. Connors, the woman at the helm of the Brain Injury Association of America. Her preference is that they all be called brain injuries.

A fourteen-year-old girl bumping her head and a 21-year-old collegian crushing his skull in a death-defying plunge have one thing in common— traumatic brain injury. Concussions aren't always treated as if they belong in that category, but they are and the cumulative effect of multiple concussions may result in similar symptoms resulting in chronic brain injury. It may be immediate or delayed, as is too often the case with boxers and football players years after their careers are over.

A lot of the things the brain can do, and the efficiency with which we respond through thought, speech and action, are regulated by a unique circuitry or how we are wired. That wiring, as if ordained by a higher power, may be rerouted from a part of the brain that doesn't work to a part that does.

Approximately half of severely head-injured patients will need surgery to remove or repair hematomas or contusions, and there are often injuries to other parts of the body, including internal organs, to address. It often means numerous surgeries, some involving the brain and others not, as was the case with C.B. They can be virtually ongoing, governed by which is more critical—a treatment triage approach, if you will. TBI almost always means that swelling occurs and fluids build in the skull, increasing intracranial pressure (ICP). There is simply no room for the brain to escape the squeeze of the skull. The previously mentioned "crumple zone" of C.B.'s skull, the way it was damaged may have actually allowed his swollen brain some of the room it needed to expand. In other words, the nature of the injury itself, in all of its devastation, may have been instrumental in C.B.'s subsequent healing.

Neurosurgeons are adherents of the Monro-Kellie hypothesis, which states that there is a fixed amount of space inside the skull to accommodate the sum of the volume of blood, brain tissue and cerebrospinal fluid (CSF). Decompressive craniectomy, or removing part of the skull vault that encases the swollen brain, is now commonly used to relieve ICP. Various approaches to freezing or cooling the brain are also used. These were not options for C.B. Miller back in 1994.

"The first time we saw C.B. was when they were taking him in for surgery. He was not conscious and his head was beginning to swell," his father, Mike recalls. "When he came out of this surgery I could not believe how big his head seemed..."

"The visual that I remember most clearly was seeing him propped up in his bed in the I.C.U. and seeing just how intensely swollen his head was...." sister, Kathie, recalls, an image that remains vivid in her memory. "Words can't really describe it. I remember thinking his head must be about three times its normal size. Then immediately dismissing it and thinking that's not possible."

Later, after the swelling went down and the ICP crisis, measured by a cranial bolt, had passed, seeing the gap between the head and neck brace, reinforced to her "just how outrageous it (swelling) had been..." The family would be, as Kathie puts it, "obsessed" by the

ICP readings over the first few days and she recalls readings reaching five times the normal pressure levels. The cranial bolt is essentially a catheter, a hollow bolt, inserted into the brain with sensors that measure the internal pressure in the swelling and traumatized brain.

Healing and growing, with room to fail

Today, it is common to cut away part of the skull, as they did with Gabby Giffords when she suffered massive head injuries. The idea is that doing so makes more room for the brain to swell as a result of the initial trauma, without bumping up against the confinement of the skull cavity. Hitting against the inside of the skull could cause further damage to the brain.

C.B. virtually destroyed the frontal left of his brain, much of the left hemisphere of the cerebral cortex, the so-called grey matter of the brain. A massive number of cells had already been destroyed, never to be regenerated, and it would be weeks before healing would take precedence over survival. The fact that there would be recovery is somewhat miraculous, and the broken skull itself may have allowed grotesque swelling, negating pressure that should have been fatal.

Did the nature of C.B.'s injuries somehow serve him well in the absence of the now commonly practiced decompressive craniectomy? It's difficult to know. In retrospect, Michael Miller, the doctor, believes that much of the swelling was external, the crushed skull and facial bones, and not primarily the brain itself. Obviously, the elevated ICP readings showed that there was dramatic brain swelling, but his brother's survival indicates that there were other forces at work.

Kathie recalls how her father, despite the prospect of being inundated by what lay ahead for C.B., always seemed to be on a steady course, with a moral compass that never wavered.

There was considerable theory at the time that what you got back in a year was all you were going to get back. Mike Miller was not willing to accept this restrictive scenario, which was geared to sparing patients from the prospects of failure. It seemed like the kind, compassionate thing to do, what with all the frustrations of recovering from traumatic injury to the brain. However, as a research chemist with a passion for learning all he could about any challenges or stumbling blocks he encountered, he would subsequently discover an approach known as the person-controlled model, that confirmed his belief that failure isn't necessarily a destructive thing. The thing about life— and perhaps what you learn the most from it— is that failure is not only a common thing. It can be a constructive thing. Why should people recovering from TBI approach life any differently?

Failure is not the end of a road. It is merely a change of direction. You make the turn and you keep going. The Millers would learn that for someone with a brain injury, just as for anyone else, failure can be a learning —and healing— experience for all involved. As an athlete, C.B. was aware that a mistake on the field of play was a lesson to be learned. The only difference was that this play was deadly serious.

The healing of the human brain, regaining lost functions resulting from injury to the brain, is known as neurologic recovery. Many brain scientists in the months, even years, following C.B.'s fall from that balcony espoused that neurologic recovery was complete in one year. Others believed it could span two or more years.

"This is hogwash," Connors preaches today on behalf of her national organization. "Recovery spans a lifetime."

There is, first, metabolic recovery of the brain tissue, which should be complete by the year anniversary of the injury, but this only paves the way for future recovery. Now the gospel of neurologic recovery is that we all have the capacity to learn throughout our lifetime, and that includes people with TBI

Mike Miller was never willing to put caps on his son's recovery, even though it flaunted conventional wisdom at the time. Not only has his approach proven to be effective, but his choices for C.B.'s rehabilitation, which is essentially lifelong learning, has become the conventional wisdom of our time.

CHAPTER 3

AFTER THE FALL: FIRST COMES SURVIVAL

On the evening of C.B.'s fall, Mike Miller was home in Towanda after dropping his younger son off in Wilkes-Barre a few hours earlier. Mike decided to turn in for the night around 11 p.m. Little did he know that C.B. was already fighting for his life in the back of an ambulance some 65 miles away.

Sharon was still up, reading, when the call came in. It was a few minutes past midnight, as she recalls, on July 22. The caller was Jack Swearhart, his nervous words tumbling together, propelled by the mixture of urgency and dread of someone bearing bad news.

"Mrs. Miller, this is Jack, C.B.'s roommate. C.B. fell off a balcony and he's unconscious. They took him to the hospital..." Sharon was trying to put together everything Jack was telling her: a balcony, and there was something about a broken railing...

The hospital, Wilkes-Barre General, was fortunately only a few minutes away from where C.B. fell. He was there at the hospital, as were Jack and a number of friends, including childhood friend and fellow Wilkes student and athlete, Jamie Wecker. Wecker knew the Millers well and had been unable to bring himself to make the call. He had been on that balcony when it happened, standing near the same railing just minutes before C.B.

Sharon did not know any of this at the time, and all she could think to ask was whether her son was still unconscious. When told he was, she awakened her sleeping husband, phone in hand. Mike was still groggy, his expression a combination of confusion and alarm. After handing him the phone, Sharon remembers the horror in his voice. "Oh, my God, Jack!" he blurted out several times as he, unknowingly, was entering an intimate relationship with traumatic brain injury that would change the course of his life.

As for Mike, he remembers the phone ringing, but only once. He was partially awake, not thinking clearly. Probably a wrong number or Sharon was talking to someone. For some reason, it didn't register that it was pretty late for anyone to be calling. Then came the sound of Sharon scurrying up the steps, her barging into the room with the phone to her ear. "Here, Jack, I need you to tell it to his father," she was saying, handing Mike the phone. The voice on the other end anxiously informed him that C.B. had fallen from a balcony and was now in the emergency room.

Mike, stunned and trying to take it all in, was picturing the balcony in a movie theater, for some reason, and trying to figure out why C.B. had been to a movie instead of going to work that afternoon. It took a few minutes for him to understand what his son's roommate was trying to tell him. Then came the sudden impact of what had happened. The fall had been head-first from a third-floor apartment balcony.

As is his nature, Mike needed to know what he would be facing. More importantly what was C.B. up against? Despite a burgeoning anxiety approaching panic, he was able to learn from Swearhart that C.B. had indeed worked into the evening and, afterward, had gone to a friend's apartment for a gathering. He and some others were enjoying the late-night air out on a porch of some sort when C.B. backed up against the railing. It gave way and he fell the full three floors, landing on the left side of his head. Mike was assured there were no drugs or alcohol involved, on C.B.'s part at least, and he had only been there a few minutes when the railing gave way. It was an accident waiting to happen, and C. B. had simply been in the wrong place at the wrong time.

Quickly apprising Sharon, they awakened their younger daughter, Kathie, who was home after completing her Bachelor's degree at Penn State University and just weeks away from reporting to graduate school in the fall at American University in Washington, D.C.

"I had a job that summer so I went to bed to get my rest," recalls Kathie, now living and working in Washington D.C. "I can still clearly remember my mom as this dark silhouette standing in the doorway of my bedroom telling me they had just gotten the call and they were going to the hospital. I said, 'I'm coming with you,' and then I remember throwing on the fastest clothes I could find, getting downstairs and getting in the car."

Meanwhile, her father was calling son, Michael, in Philadelphia and daughter, Maurie, in Elmira, NY, to tell them what had happened. Michael told his father that he would call the hospital to see what he could find out and not to leave until he heard from him.

Earlier in the preceding evening, Michael and his girlfriend at the time had gone to see a movie about a man who succeeded despite what appeared to be severe limitations. The movie was "Forrest Gump," and another character, Lieutenant Dan, had survived and, ultimately thrived, despite terrible injuries. After getting that call from his father in the early-morning hours, Michael, in turn, called the E.R. physician at Wilkes-Barre General. The young intern introduced himself as Dr. Miller to the E.R. physician at the time and learned C.B. had been unconscious when he arrived by ambulance and remained so. His first question was whether his brother was intubated, his airway cleared via insertion of a tube into his windpipe. This is an essential first step in any trauma management scenario.

This was important to know in order to proceed with any discussion on where C.B. would go from there. Knowing the size of his brother and the extent of the facial fractures, it could have made the airway very difficult to manage. "If you don't have an airway, you don't have a patient," is his candid assessment.

"You gotta understand there are two gears for me. There's a gear where I'll stop to think about it and fall apart, and there's a part of me that sees you or anyone else who comes under my medical care, and you're just an engine, like a damaged car, and I'm going to put you back together," he says today of his own ability to focus on a patient as a doctor. "It's not personal. It's mechanical… It takes more for me to lock to that level for a family member, but when my head goes to that, it's all business."

This would figure into the doctor he would become and the critical role he would ultimately play as an intermediary between his family and the medical staff:

"Part of it was having a respect for my own limitations, what I did and didn't know. I'm a physician, but there are those with a more worldly level of experience, at Wilkes-Barre General or any good hospital, and respecting what I don't know is important too... You listen and let them do what they are supposed to be doing and making sure your checklist is being addressed."

"You start being a detriment to your family member's care when you start being an ass. You don't get compassion from other people when you're an ass."

"It does not sound good"

It was only a matter of minutes—minutes that must have seemed interminable for the distraught parents in Towanda—until Mike Miller got that call back from his elder son. Other than C.B. still being alive, it was not welcome news: "Dad, you better get down to Wilkes-Barre as quick as you can. It does not sound good."

Years later, reflecting on that night—the minutes, hours, weeks, months and years that would intervene— Mike sees it as a bittersweet new beginning:

"So we embarked on a journey that would really last from that date to the present time. The drive that night, of one and a half hours, seemed in ways to go instantly, but in others it seemed like a lifetime. During the trip I believe that I lived through all of the possible scenarios that one could imagine."

"I can recall that night pretty clearly,," Kathie recalls. "I remember driving through Meshoppen (known to be a speed trap). I remember

Dad saying, 'I don't care. They can stop me if they want to.'" During the drive, though the tension was thick, Kathie quizzed her parents for information, trying to get up to speed about what was going on. "I could tell it was a pretty grave situation. ...Come to think of it, that's a very unfortunate word."

Maurie was in the process of moving from her apartment in Elmira at the time. She was packing and didn't get to bed until about 2:30 a.m. She had barely fallen asleep, sometime around 3 a.m., when she was awakened by a call from home. She was advised to stay where she was for the time being. Later that day, July 22nd, she would get a ride to Wilkes-Barre with her uncle and aunt, J. Ed and Mary Jo Miller. Unable to sleep, she stayed up all night packing. She was having some issues with her landlords about the moving process. Their reaction to the family tragedy would be "less than understanding."

"Getting to the hospital was a blur," Maurie remembers. "There was so much uncertainty about what was happening."

The first time the Millers saw C.B. at Wilkes-Barre General was when they were taking him in for surgery. His head was beginning to grow noticeably. When they wheeled him out of the initial surgery his head had swollen dramatically, almost to the point of being surreal.

"He had a neck collar on but his head looked so big that the collar seemed inadequate to contain the swelling," his father recalls. "He had tubes connected to a number of places and was on machines that not only monitored his vital signs but were, at this time breathing for him."

His mother says that when they finally did get to see him, the only movement was a slight movement of his legs. His eyes looked like "purple golf balls" and his lips were so swollen they didn't seem real.

Here is where Michael was invaluable. The doctors were grimly concerned about C.B.'s condition, and they could be straightforward, sometimes brutally honest, with him. He, in turn, would keep his parents and sisters in the loop. It was a matter of survival for the young patient, as his father notes:

"The first critical period was 24 hours. Once he survived this, they then said that 48 hours was critical. Then 72. I remember feeling that we should celebrate like it was his birthday when he reached the 72nd hour. He was kept in a drug-induced coma for the next two weeks. After this he remained comatose for two to three weeks more. It is not easy to say when a person is really out of a coma. Consciousness returns slowly."

And so the survival watch continued. Staying alive was the priority, but what were the chances of Christopher Bradley Miller ever living a useful life again, let alone approaching what had once been a promising future?

C.B. would be at Wilkes-Barre General over the next three months. The number of surgeries he would undergo would eventually total fourteen. He doesn't remember any of it. Some might say it was the lost summer of his life.

C.B. doesn't see it that way. To him it was the birthing process for a whole new life, and, like the time in the womb, there is little, if anything, to remember.

CHAPTER 4

GUARDIAN ANGELS AND CRUMPLE ZONES

Sharon Miller was in for the long haul from the start. Aside from sleeping and tending to basic needs, she was tethered to that hospital, as close as she could be to her unconscious son, for months. It started in the early morning hours of July 22, 1994, when they arrived at Wilkes-Barre General. It was about 3:30 in the morning. They were wheeling C.B. into his first surgery, mostly exploratory to determine the extent of the damage to the skull, as well as dealing with some facial issues and inserting the cranial bolt.

Seeing his grossly swollen head and "purple golf ball" eyes shouldn't have made her feel particularly hopeful, but, despite fear bordering on terror, she convinced herself he was going to be all right. For starters, he was still alive and that meant he had already beaten some steep odds. They would soon learn from C.B.'s friends about Stefan Clausen having the presence to turn his head and clear the airway in the minutes before the ambulance arrived. She was —and still is—so thankful he had been there. Sharon believes in the power of prayer and, with a son as a doctor and faith that God was looking out for them, was very trusting in the care C.B. was being given.

Kathie, who accompanied her parents to the hospital that morning, remembers trying to process all the information about the skull fractures and brain damage. Hospital staff took Mike, Sharon and Kathie up to see C.B. before he went into surgery. They rode in the same elevator used to transport the patients. When the doors opened "I could see blood on the floor in kind of a repeating pattern, like it had been from the wheels of a gurney... a trail of blood." Upon seeing this, Kathie immediately hoped her mother wasn't seeing it. "I couldn't help but think that blood trail had been left by C.B., and I didn't want that thought to tear her up like it was tearing me up."

Mike, Sharon and Kathie had a chance to see C.B. briefly as he was transferred to surgery. They each stood by the side of the gurney and reassured him that they were there for him. The next time they would see C.B. was after surgery, once he was placed in the I.C.U. "They told us he would be paralyzed due to drugs they were using," says Kathie of the initial consultation with doctors. Paralytic drugs have assorted uses, including helping patients remain still after an injury.

Yet when the family actually got to see C.B. minutes later, they noticed his body move. They all saw it, and it was something they hadn't expected. It seemed as if he were somehow reacting to the sound of their voices. When they started to talk, his legs and arms began to move. At first, this was reassuring. Then, as they would discover in the roller-coaster pattern of T.B.I. recovery, hopefulness turned to concern. Should he be doing this? Were the drugs working?

Most of these kinds of worries were spared the family, because of the doctor among them. Michael, the son, would arrive from Philadelphia shortly after the rest of his family.

"My most important role was to help my parents negotiate through what was happening. I understood full well the gravity of it to the point that I actually talked to the transplant people (about getting C.B.'s healthy organs to others if he didn't make it)," he explains. "I was already thinking that his life could make a difference in multiple peoples' lives."

This was not something his parents needed to face at that time, though it was the positive alternative to leaving everything in that room if C.B. were to die. Nevertheless, he did explain this to them, knowing that they might resent this extra dose of negativity in what were already emotionally debilitating circumstances. He did get their approval to make the call, putting transplant people on notice, but the impact of this decision struck home with a powerful punch when the kidney donor nurse arrived and took him aside.

"I cried, flat out just lost it after talking with her," he says, temporarily reverting to loving brother from his doctor persona. "In a way it was actually very therapeutic." With this release of emotion, he reclaimed his professional detachment. He knew he had to be careful to keep his emotions in check in front of his parents. Seeing him overly concerned would amplify their own fears.

Where Michael, the son, was practical and prepared for all the contingencies, Mike, the father, was hanging his hat on hope and the power of prayer and positive energy. His son's immediate fate was in the hands of others. His talents and determination would come into play later.

So hopeful was Sharon that she started keeping a journal, addressing the entries to C.B., knowing that he would get to read them some day and fill in the missing gaps in his destroyed memory. She was not ready to deal with the real possibility that, even if he survived, her youngest son may never even be capable of reading that journal or even comprehend its contents.

"When it was first mentioned about where he would go [when he was able to leave the hospital], I can remember thinking to myself, 'If he survives we will take him home!' I just had no clue as to what was ahead of us," Sharon would confess years later when sharing their story. "I soon realized it would be like taking home a 200-pound newborn. He was not able to do anything for himself."

In the meantime, the priority was on survival and C.B. definitely was not alone.

"The waiting room is like a Miller campground," his mother noted in her journal, referring to a slew of his buddies, both from Towanda and Wilkes, who "are in and out." There were also friends of the family and relatives. Some seemed to be there continually. Others dropped by when they could. All were devastated and comforting each other as they awaited each piece of news, each update, about whether C.B. was going to make it. Those who had seen him, lying there bleeding on a slab of flagstone, wondered if it was even possible to survive such injuries. If they entertained such doubts, they kept them to themselves, revealing them only in relief after the crisis had passed.

There was plenty of crying together, bonding of the most intimate kind, and sharing of deepest feelings. Doctors would come in with reassuring words about C.B.'s immediate progress, yet at the same time urge friends and family to bolster themselves for the trials ahead. Sharon retains vivid images of people of all ages, young and old, in and out, sitting on the floor. All-night vigils continued through the critical 72-hour span, but the visitors, the campers, were there for weeks throughout the coma.

Deep inside, the healing begins

They were learning, even just days after the fall, that they would have plenty of help handling what needed to be done. On July 23, they returned to their home in Towanda to pack some things. They arrived to find friends and neighbors with riding and push mowers tending to their spacious lawn.

"What a sight!" Sharon says.

"Now that is a lawn that was mowed with love," was Maurie's reaction.

At the hospital, with each milestone of survival, the mood of the "campground" became increasingly positive. There was even laughter. Just sharing stories about C.B. was enough to do that. As time went on, with C.B. virtually unresponsive in his bed, the mood in his room was, well, cheery at times. It was as if C.B. were hosting a party, but somewhere, deep inside that unresponsive body and battered brain, healing was taking place.

C.B. says he has murky recollections of the voices of people talking when he was in a coma. Those three months in the hospital are mostly lost to his memory, though he recalls not being physically able to respond to voices around him. He also recalls that there was this strange sense of well-being.

"It was not unusual to go to the room and hear spirited conversation and laughter," says his father of those weeks that C.B. was in a coma, gradually responding to outside stimuli.

"C.B.'s college friends came and went on a regular basis, telling us wonderful C.B. stories," says Sharon. "Some would sit by his bed and pray while others would tell him what was happening in their world. We told everyone to talk to him, not about him, when they were in his room."

It was as if C.B. was there, taking part in the fellowship. Mike and Sharon returned from the cafeteria after taking a break one day, knowing that a group of C.B.'s friends was keeping him company. They could hear laughing and animated discussion as they approached the room, giving them fleeting hope that C.B. had miraculously regained consciousness. As they entered the room, Mike noticed some shuffling, something being passed around the room, and caught a fleeting glimpse of a Playboy magazine being tucked away.

"I don't know what therapeutic method they used with this magazine, but I do know that the atmosphere in that room, with C.B. in a coma and hooked up to more machines than I could describe, was very positive," Mike concluded.

That's the way it was. Accentuating the positive, trying to trigger something in that dormant brain, whether it be prayers, one-sided conversations or Playboys. It included hours on end of reading to him, holding his hand, touching, talking and never talking about him as if he weren't there.

One of the books they would share reading, as C.B. lay unresponsive in the hospital all those days and weeks, was "Rise & Walk," the triumphant story of Dennis Byrd, defensive end for the New York Jets in the early 1990's. Byrd sustained a neck injury in a game against the Kansas City Chiefs on November 29, 1992, rendering him paralyzed and unable to walk. It brought an end to his NFL career, but Byrd inspired an entire nation when he appeared at the Jets' opening home game of the 1993 season as honorary captain. Byrd had defied the odds with his comeback, and it seemed a fitting story to share with their unconscious son. Like Byrd, C.B.'s life may never return to what it had been prior to his accident, but it could still be fulfilling and meaningful.

In a sense, they were already putting him on the comeback trail, even with all the uncertainties—lingering issues of life and death— that prevailed.

The first two or three days ran together, as if there were no distinction between night and day. In some ways it seemed like night all the time, as it had been when he fell from the balcony. Over the span of 48 hours C.B was examined by a battery of specialists. The head injuries were obviously extensive, but the good news was that C.B. had sustained minimal physical damage otherwise. That, in itself, was miraculous, considering how far he had fallen. There was a broken wrist to mend and a bruised kidney to heal. Elsewhere on his face, he had broken both his upper and lower jaws. There were some concerns about neck injury initially, but there were apparently no back injuries. Again, if not a miracle, it was a blessing that his back, and his neck, as it turned out, would not require surgery.

One of the early problems in figuring out what other injuries might be present was the inability to get an acceptable x-ray. C.B.'s massive frame and broad shoulders made this a challenge. The solution was to put the former high school swimming standout into what is known as the swimmer's position, requiring one arm to be fully extended like a pitcher just releasing a fast ball and the trailing arm to be lowered behind. However, concerns about the intracranial pressure exerted by tissue and cerebral spinal fluid on his battered brain prohibited this.

To be candid, they didn't know as much about T.B.I. in 1994 as they would even just a decade later. In fact, the basic treatment would change. The surgeons and staff at Wilkes-Barre General did an amazing job and the results speak for themselves, but, in many ways, they did it the old-fashioned way.

Craniectomy, or cutting away a section of the skull to relieve the intracranial pressure, was not part of the procedure at the time. That became standard procedure after the Iraq and Afghanistan hostilities. Wars, whatever their other consequences, teach us how to efficiently deal with people with critical injuries, whether it be to body, brain or psyche. The greatest advances in treating this injury prior to that came out of Vietnam a quarter century before.

The technology in 1994 was hyperventilation, plenty of oxygen and then managing responses to intracranial pressure. They put C.B.'s brain into a phenobarbital coma, an induced deep coma, which as Michael explains is "a very deep level of sedation that allows his neurological activity to go away… you pharmacologically make him brain dead."

That helps the brain repair itself. They now take measures to help with decompression cooling the brain and removing chunks of the skull that will be reattached later. They relied on none of those options for C.B. during those dark days of July of 1994.

Emotions collide, bringing acceptance

Meanwhile, Mike will never forget the roller coaster of emotions. For a guy who knows how to get things done and achieve goals, the only thing he could do was let the doctors do their jobs, consulting his namesake regarding any immediate decisions that might have to be made in terms of C.B.'s care.

"There were a number of times that my prayers gave me strength that I did not realize I had. There were an almost infinite number of times that I had this feeling of inadequacy, but relying on my faith and the support of our loving friends and family got me through them all."

The feeling of helplessness was the worst part. Despite his faith in God as a devout Catholic, he did have to stem the welling anger, the sense of unfairness, prompted by the question of why God would allow this to happen to C.B. The weary parents continued their all-night vigils at the hospital until three days later, on the 25th. That is when they got to spend their first night away in a nearby hotel room. Mike was exhausted but unable to sleep. While in the shower, flooded internally by conflicting emotions as the warm water poured over him, Mike came to terms with himself and with his God. For the first time, he surrendered to a wellspring of emotions and let himself go.

"As I stood there I thought that there was no way I could handle all of what faced us. But I began to think about how the God I believed in all of my life had come to the aid of others. I thought of Abraham when he was ordered to sacrifice his only son. As he started to deliver the fatal blow, he was told not to do it. At this point I realized that I could do nothing directly to affect the outcome of C.B.'s injuries. The outcome of his situation was up to a much higher power than me."

It was then that the anger gave way to acceptance of a situation that was beyond his control. He knew he would need strength for whatever lay ahead and he turned to prayer:

"If C.B. were to live, I prayed that God would give me strength and guidance to be able to handle all of the challenges. I also pledged that I would work on the challenges with all of my energy. If he were to die, I prayed that God would help me to handle that also."

Early that next morning, July 26th, Mike and Sharon were in bed, but awake and talking, in their hotel room when there was a knock at the door.

"Just a second!" Mike called out as he quickly put on some clothes. When he opened the door just seconds later, there was nobody there and the hall was empty. The incident spurred them into getting up, showering and being ready well before the alarm clock would have called them to action. Just as they were about to leave, the hotel room phone rang. It was their doctor son, Michael, calling to urge them to get to the hospital as quickly as possible to sign papers.

Sharon remembers they could barely hear him because he "was so upset and torn." It was a rare betrayal of emotion from their elder son, but it seemed that even he was nearing a breaking point.

The reason for urgency: C.B. was developing blood clots. They needed to implant a Greenfield Filter out of concern that a clot might fatally dislodge. Every second counted, but they could not proceed with the surgery without signed permission.

"Had it not been for that knock on the door, we wouldn't have been ready to walk out the door and head straight for the hospital when Michael called," Sharon says. She goes on to agree with an observation made by a friend about that mysterious knock: "It must have been an angel."

The Greenfield Filter, also known as the inferior vena cava (IVC) filter, is generally shaped like a badminton shuttlecock. It is implanted when there is a high risk of pulmonary embolism (PE), which increases the probability of sudden death. Depending on where clots are forming, it is usually inserted via the femoral (groin) or internal jugular (neck) vein. This device would catch any blood clots in the deep veins and prevent them from lodging in the lungs or the brain. Without this filter, with blood clots forming the way they were, they would be playing Russian roulette with C.B.'s life.

About 60,000 people die every year from pulmonary embolism, caused by deep-vein thrombosis, according to the American Heart Association. Some ten times that many are hospitalized to treat the condition, and the stents of the Greenfield Filter are often the lifesavers, catching those grenades before they blow up a vital organ.

"You sure gave us a scare to start the day," Sharon tells C.B, in her journal, "but it got better!"

A miracle in the making

During those first few weeks, and throughout C.B.'s three-month stay at Wilkes-Barre General, there was progress, but it often seemed incredibly slow. Aside from the scare from the blood clots, there were the wiring of his jaws and the setting of his broken wrist. He also seemed to get a string of infections (one in his injured eye, a number of kidney and bladder infections and others). It was eventually determined that, because of damage in his head, he needed a Ventriculoperitoneal (VP) shunt between his brain ventrical and peritoneal cavity (stomach), diverting cerebrospinal fluid. This surgery could not be done until all of the infections had been resolved.

Then there was the relentless concern during those first few days over the intracranial pressure (ICP) readings measured by the cranial bolt. The readings that sister Kathie mentioned the family "obsessed" over, watching for any changes, good or bad.

This might have been more disheartening to the family, if not for the fact that their spirits were continually nourished by the prayers and support they received from C.B.'s college community in Wilkes-Barre, as well as the family's church and community of friends back home in Towanda.

Jane Lampe-Groh, Dean of Student Affairs at Wilkes University, was there from the beginning. In fact, she was one of the first to greet the Millers when they arrived at the hospital in the hours following the accident. Lampe-Groh would later cite the miracle of C.B.'s comeback to the next graduating class of nursing students at Wilkes. The response of Wilkes students and faculty was impressive, but as Lampe-Groh pointed out in that speech, so was that of Wilkes alumni. They included the first police officer to respond to the scene, a number of the nurses who cared for him, and the neurosurgeon who would eventually take on his case.

As the family closely monitored the situation it didn't take long for C.B.'s oldest sibling to question the advice they were getting from the neurosurgeon who had been on-call and initially assigned to C.B.'s case. Even as a fresh-faced doctor, an intern working an emergency room in Philadelphia, Michael felt that the specialist in charge seemed to have the attitude that it was a lost cause, that he would allow C.B. to go gently into the night rather than attempt any drastic measures that might not only save C.B.'s life but also give his brother a better chance of recovering, possibly even to a point of approaching the person he had been.

"I knew realistically that there was no shot at 100 percent (recovery), but from that first night my goal was that he would be 85 percent of what he was a year from then," explained Michael. At the time, the outlook for people with traumatic brain injury essentially indicated that most of what they would regain occurred within a year after injury. Destroyed brain cells don't come back to life, and there is only so much the rest of the brain can do to make up the difference. Fortunately, so much can sometimes be a lot.

The neurosurgeon initially assigned to C.B.'s case applied a strategy that utilized a relatively light drug-induced coma and monitored for seizures. Michael was not comfortable with this approach and began to investigate alternatives.

"My sense was that he was just going to watch my brother go. It was as though he determined there was nothing to do – it was just a bad accident," is how Michael characterized his feelings at the time. Turning to someone whom he trusted and respected, Michael decided he would find another neurosurgeon who might be willing to take over. He did, and that specialist would be Dr. David Sedor.

"That was a big step for an intern just a couple of weeks into his post medical school career," Michael said of his decision to change neurosurgeons at this critical juncture.

Within 48 hours of C.B.'s fall, Dr. Sedor would take over and apply a more aggressive strategy. At 21, C.B. had age working in his favor. As a college athlete already prepared for pre-season football practice, he also had physical strength. Dr. Sedor saw these two traits as benefitting C.B. and the options he might use to heal him. He ultimately deepened the drug-induced coma, essentially using the drugs to render C.B. brain dead. Kathie recalls that Dr. Sedor described it to the family like this: "When you sprain your ankle, the doctor tells you to stay off your ankle, and you can do that by not walking for a few days. Well, imagine that C.B. has sprained his brain. The way to get C.B. off his brain so it can heal is to administer these drugs."

By the 29th of July, a little more than a week after the accident, they started cutting back on the drugs that were keeping C.B. in a deep coma. ICP readings were going down, no longer spiking. The relief was palpable, but everyone knew C.B. was not entirely out of the woods just yet. The family would continue to grapple with a complex mix of emotions, ranging from feeling a sense of promise and hope, to being riddled with worry and frustrations.

"Some days I would wake up and sit wondering how long I could go on holding his lifeless hand, but somehow I found the strength to go on," Mike, the father, would later comment.

On a quick trip back to Towanda on Aug. 3, it seemed that even the skies were venting anger and frustration. A thunderstorm rumbled outside while Mike and Sharon were in the house, grabbing some items to take back to Wilkes-Barre, where they now had a place to stay other than a hotel room Maurie, the family caretaker, had arranged for them. It seemed the storm had passed, but as Mike scurried outside to load the car, a bolt of lightning blasted a nearby pine tree, freezing him in terror for just a second.

There are omens all around, or so it may seem, but how do you interpret them? Had they paused to contemplate such things, would they conclude that the forces of nature were beyond their control or that they would survive the storm, no matter how close it came to striking them down?

Bolstered by "a huge sense of peace"

It had been a harrowing handful of days that must have seemed like a lifetime. There had been so many crossroads on the first leg of the journey—just keeping C.B. alive—but both of his sisters say they knew he would somehow make it, despite the seemingly steep odds against him doing so.

Maurie had seen her youngest brother and heard the prognoses before having to return to Elmira to complete the move from her apartment. It was not something she wanted to do, leaving her family at that critical juncture, but it was something that circumstances dictated. When she got back to her rented abode there was "a whole clan of people at the apartment to move me. We took out a window to get my furniture out of the house, because they just wanted it to get done lickety-split. I have never been moved so fast in my life… It was a whirlwind, and all of a sudden I was by myself in my new apartment."

Deprived of sleep and somewhat disoriented by this time, she stayed in Elmira that night before returning to Wilkes-Barre the next morning. She had received a call from her parents that night saying C.B. was not doing so well. Maurie's move happened to occur at the same time those blood clots were posing a threat to C.B.'s survival. All alone and knowing her brother was hovering close to death, she had this comforting feeling that everything was going to be all right.

"I am a woman of faith and there was a huge sense of peace that came over me that night that I will never forget," she recalled. She enjoyed the healing sleep of the untroubled.

Kathie, too, sensed from the start that C.B. was going to be okay, even as they made the initial drive to Wilkes-Barre. Most of the time, during those first few days, they were in the immediate moment, dealing with what was going on right then. When she did allow her thoughts to skip ahead, however, there was a feeling of well-being.

She had bought C.B. a necklace for his birthday when he turned 21 barely two months before the fall. They had to cut it off him and returned it, along with other belongings, to the family. Each kept something of his; Kathie kept the necklace.

"I would hold the necklace and talk to him. It was my form of prayer," she remembered. "Most of the time, I would say something along the lines of 'you need energy right now and I've got a lot of it. Take whatever you need from me.' Here comes the part I can't quite explain. When C.B. went in for a procedure, I was in the waiting room… and

I basically don't remember anything for about a 45- to 60-minute period.... One minute, I was doing my thing, telling him to take my energy. The next, I was out, unconscious, I guess. Then, all of a sudden I was wide awake, and sat up. I had been lying on the couch. Seconds later, the doctor came in and said C.B. had made it through the procedure and everything was fine.... I'm not a religious person, but something happened there, It is still something I can't explain."

It was the morning they had to insert the Greenfield Filter to thwart a deadly pulmonary embolism. She stops short of saying her prayer or meditation may have energized C.B. in some way through this delicate stage. "If pushed, I might use the word 'miracle.'"

This comes from a skeptic. Kathie does not adhere to an organized religion and has questioned the teachings of her Catholic upbringing and the existence of a higher power since college. Maurie, on the other hand, accepted her faith without question, as she does now. Each, following her own compass, had found a spiritual connection to her brother, a soothing certainty that he would emerge from this nightmare and find a path in life.

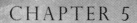

CHAPTER 5

SMALL STEPS AND THEN A ROADBLOCK

C.B.'s recovery featured some dramatic moments at Wilkes-Barre General Hospital, but there was also a lot of uncertainty about just how far he could come back. He would be there three months, an entire summer of his life, spending a good half of that time in a coma, induced and natural. He doesn't remember any of it. In fact, his first lucid memory would be in an ambulance when he left the hospital, transferring him to a rehabilitation center and the second crucial leg of his journey.

After nearly six weeks in the hospital, C.B. was slowly regaining consciousness. Small victories were in abundance along the way, hinting that the old C.B. was still in there somewhere. One of the most dramatic came from a simple gesture most of us take for granted.

A close friend of C.B.'s, Robin Orendorff, was visiting one day. C.B. had been starting to react with his eyes and facial expressions, but body movement was sporadic and incidental. Up until that time, the only purposeful movement of his limbs came with the assistance of physical therapists. With their help, he was walking. Without it, however, he did very little. As Robin ended her visit and said good-bye that day, C.B. pulled up his left arm—the good one— and responded with what was clearly a wave. Overjoyed, Robin ran off to tell C.B.'s parents, who, in turn, celebrated. For them, this simple wave, this voluntary, self-directed move was a significant milestone along the path of what they knew would be a continued recovery.

It was a moment worthy of the record books. For her part, Sharon noted it in her journal, adding that, after Robin left, C.B. applauded himself, giving them a hand on command. Later, this story was reported in Wilkes University student newspaper, The Beacon on Sept. 8, 1994. The incident of the wave was recounted as part of a feature article that described C.B. as "a true fighting spirit." A fighting spirit indeed, C.B. was connecting his brain and his body. Slowly, he was returning to full consciousness mode.

Contributing to this milestone moment was the therapy that C.B. received while in the hospital. Occupational and physical therapy started barely a month after he was brought into the hospital and only a day after he was taken off the respirator. The treatment was clearly proactive, even if his response was minimal, and it seemed to be igniting sparks in that massively impaired brain. Technically, C.B. was still in a coma, but he was responding to voices. And he was moving so much in his bed that it was difficult to keep the covers on him. In her journal on Aug. 23, C.B.'s mother described the formerly unresponsive hulk that was her son as "active and looking devilish."

Devilish they gladly accepted, along with any angels that came along. While the family still grappled with the uncertainties of the situation, not knowing precisely what the future might hold for C.B. or who might emerge from the coma, there were clear signs of hope – Hope that the C.B. they had known and loved for 21 years was still in there, finding his way back.

During their time with him, the therapists would stand C.B. up to clean him, firing off more neurons. The semi-conscious patient—shrunken from his previous bulk, though still imposing—was put through a solid two hours of physical and occupational therapy on Aug. 26, a mere five weeks after the fall. The rigorous exercise was just a sampling of what was to come.

His movements were small at first. Then C.B. was tossing and turning, as if he was trying to get out of bed by throwing his good left leg over the side. While it seemed his body was beginning to reconnect, there was little to no indication that he knew either of his parents. They would watch as hospital staff rolled C.B. off to therapy sessions in a wheelchair,. They watched as it took four people to stand him up and move him around.

"I can still remember the thrill I felt the first day I witnessed him taking a step, even though it was with a lot of assistance," says his father. "I had returned from work early and found his bed empty when I got to his room. The nurse told me that they had taken him down for therapy. So I went to the therapy area and sat with Sharon as they got C.B. up to take a few steps. How thrilling!"

Just as memorable was something else that happened that day C.B. took his first step. He snapped his fingers, then reached over and tapped his father on his shirt pocket where he had just secured a roll of mints after popping one into his mouth. It was as if C.B. was saying, "Where's mine?" Since he still was not taking food orally, it was not a request Mike could honor, but it told him there was a thought process there other than basic, primal physical responses.

Putting the books back on the shelves

As the end of September approached, the wire was removed from C.B.'s mended jaw, allowing him the ability to speak. At first, he did not speak using an impressive vocabulary, but it was speech nonetheless. "I know," he said on Sept. 20 in response to some long forgotten remark. A few days later, he blurted out, "No, no, no!" More remarkably, and with some help, he was even able to write his name for the first time with his left hand. This is something he still can't do with his once dominant right hand. In fact, the skills of reading and writing would never quite be counted among the great successes of his recovery, but there would be ways around that.

"The words were few and far between at first," says Sharon, who learned that coming out of a coma is not necessarily as inspirational or dramatic as it's depicted in fictional tales. "People don't wake up like they do in the movies and say, 'Hi, Mom!'" Indeed, the process is such that there is not necessarily a specific moment when they arrive at the state of consciousness. It's more like a deep fitful sleep during which you drift in and out, seemingly responsive at times, and then dozing off at others.

C.B.'s family formulated the initial strategy for his care. Even while he was still comatose, they exposed him to constant stimuli. They would read to him every day from books and articles in the daily newspaper. They would touch, hold and rub his good hand and arm, while verbally describing what part of the limb or appendage they were touching. He was consistently being reminded who he was and various elements of his past life. As he came out of his coma, spending more and more moments in a conscious state, they showed him photos and encouraged friends who visited to be both visual and verbal. Throughout all of the stimuli, C.B. was slowly piecing things back together, like rebuilding a library after an earthquake.

Picture this: An earthquake strikes a library, knocking over shelves and leaving books in a disorganized mess. This metaphoric library is C.B.'s brain, shaken and rattled in that fall. It contains all of C.B.'s knowledge and resources, and C.B. is then tasked with working through the rubble to sort through and reorganize the thousands of books knocked off the shelves and strewn about. Compounding the job, the lighting system has been destroyed, leaving C.B. to undertake this daunting task virtually in the dark. As he struggles to put the books back in their proper places, lighting gradually returns. Progress is made, bringing more organization as well as better lighting. C.B. starts to get a better feel for what goes where. He even discovers he's put some of them back in the wrong place and re-arranges them accordingly. It's a tedious process, and it's going to take a long time to restore things to the way they were. He might even have to settle for throwing some of the resource material away because there is no shelf there for it.

This is how son, Michael, described C.B.'s plight to his father. In a way, the goal was to improve the lighting in the library, while at the same time keeping C.B. motivated to complete as much of the task as he could. Only C.B. is allowed in that library, only he can figure out how to put it back together again, but he can draw upon inspiration and instruction from the outside.

"So much was coming at us so quickly in those first few days, and he was responsible for C.B.'s care," says Kathie, noting that her father assumed the mantle as C.B.'s advocate with a stone cold urgency, at the same time dealing with the conflicting emotions of being the father of a brain-injured patient. "Yet, from the very beginning he refused to accept the status quo, or whatever it may have been, that he was being presented. He insisted on thinking everything through to make sure C.B. got what he needed. That wasn't easy at times, especially when we were presented with urgent, critical decisions, but my dad was determined. From the very start, he was determined."

Mike's dogged determination would carry through to all stages of C.B.'s case, from critical treatment to rehab to insurance coverage to financial and legal issues that would extend far beyond health-care demands into future life needs. Meanwhile, Sharon was focused on staying at C.B.'s side until he was awake and reacting. She stayed there for most of the summer, leaving only occasionally. As for Mike, there was a need to get back to work, to return to some sense of normal, to the ongoing rhythm and pattern of everyday life. Plus he had a job with an employer he felt had earned his loyalty. He needed to get away from the surreal environment of hotels and hospitals. He also needed to continue to earn a living.

A few weeks after the accident, Mike returned to work, commuting some 70 miles each way. He kept an even more tiring schedule with no wasted minutes and little time for rest and recharging. He was in a routine and taking action, not reacting to the situation as it played out.

"There were a number of times that God must have directed the car back to Wilkes-Barre, allowing me to find the strength to go for another few hours," he said of his decision to return to work and commute between Wilkes-Barre and Towanda. "I did not have the strength to deal with this situation by myself."

Returning to the ranks of the living

Whatever one might believe God's role to be in all of this, and in all of life, generosity and kindnesses abounded from the people in the lives of the Miller family. Some of it came from people they'd known for years, people of their hometown. And some of it came from people they'd never met before this tragedy brought them together. All of it mattered to the Millers more than words could ever fully express.

The summer of the accident, C.B. had been working at the Woodlands Inn, situated near Wilkes-Barre. When the family had to stay for an extended period of time, the Woodlands offered them one of the cabins they had on the property, telling the Millers they could stay there for several weeks at a reduced rate.

When Mike went to pay the bill to leave the Woodlands, it was a fraction of what it should have been. Assuming there was a mistake, he pointed this out to the clerk at the registration desk.

"Well, sir, somebody's been paying your bill," he was informed.

The Millers learned later that congregants of their church, St. Peter and Paul's in Towanda, took up a collection to help pay their lodging costs. Their priest has been delivering the donations to the Woodlands, helping to pay the bill.

When it came time to find a longer-term solution for accommodations in Wilkes-Barre, the people at Wilkes University came through with some available campus housing. Upon leaving the cabin, Mike and Sharon settled into an on-campus apartment that was typically used by visiting faculty but available at the time they needed it. The incredible generosity from the school made it possible for Sharon to stay by C.B.'s side during the day, and for both she and Mike to have a place to rest their weary heads until they could return to their home in Towanda.

C.B.'s progress continued into the fall, though he remained a man of few words. In the opening days of October, among his last at the hospital, he laboriously signs "CB" to cards of thanks being sent out to all of those who have extended prayers and well wishes.

C.B. himself, still apparently in a semiconscious state with no memory triggers, was about to return to the ranks of the living. On Oct. 5, they moved him to the John Heinz rehabilitation center, also in Wilkes-Barre. The jostling of the ambulance ride remains his first clear recollection since that lost Thursday in July. The transition from the hospital to the rehab center was an emotional milestone. His mother was moved by one of the therapists at the hospital coming to tell him good-bye and then leaving with tears in her eyes.

"We knew you were very apprehensive about the move... A very emotional day for me," Sharon writes to C.B. in her journal to him. "We had to let you go all over again."

It was tough for his Mom when she came to the rehab center the following day,, to tell him that she was going to be leaving his side for the first time in 11 weeks, that she, too, would be returning to

Towanda. She would still be seeing him several times a week, but the bond of her almost constant presence would be broken for the first time.

As she was getting ready to leave, C.B. moved her purse away from her, telling her, "No, no, no." She stayed for a while and then, some time later, cautiously asked him if he thought she should go. It would have been unbearable for her had he continued to say, "No, no, no." Instead, his demeanor softened and he shook his head affirmatively.

"I shed some tears on the way and really broke down when I got home to your dad's hug," she reported in the journal.

It was time. Mike and Sharon agreed. C.B. needed some time without them around, and they both needed to be home where they could return to a semblance of a normal life. They traveled to Wilkes-Barre at least two nights a week and, of course, sustained weekend visits. It's not as if they weren't there a lot, but it did provide some separation for C.B., who had such a long way to go on his continuing journey of recovery. Aside from the physical demands ahead, he was essentially monosyllabic when his rehabilitation began in earnest.

Donna Kopicki is still with social services at John Heinz Rehab and was C.B.'s caseworker when he was transferred from Wilkes-Barre General. Her first impression of C.B. and his chances of recovering were not particularly hopeful.

"It was going to be a long road, that was obvious," she recalled. That's about as negative as a caseworker/certified registered nurse in a brain injury unit will get, because you never know what to expect from the human brain if you can set some sparks off and get it fired up. Even in the best-case scenario you can be sure that for every great stride forward, there will be some backward steps.

The John Heinz Institute of Rehabilitation Medicine lies on the northern edge of the City of Wilkes-Barre, nestled in the sprawl of malls and commercial strip development that almost always form adjacent to metropolitan areas. Downtown Wilkes-Barre struggles to retain relevancy for those who shop, dine and seek entertainment, a losing battle fought by most American cities.

The rehab facility was named after the popular Pennsylvania senator, a young and vibrant favorite son of Pittsburgh and legitimate presidential hopeful, heir to the H.J. Heinz fortune. John Heinz had died in a freak air collision that also claimed the lives of five others barely three years before C.B.'s fall. He had dedicated his life to public service, not to the family business of making condiments for America's favorite foods, though his given name, Henry John Heinz III, and his MBA could have locked him into such a fate. As it turned out, his death and bestowals that came from it, including contributions to science, medicine and scholarship, made his name synonymous with public service and healing broken bodies. You might say his legacy was serving the underserved, many of them young, severely wounded soldiers. Then there was another army of teens and young adults, victims of the scourge of youthful America, motor vehicle accidents.

Most TBI patients being treated and rehabbed were young and male, and that was especially true at Heinz.

Accepting the Challenges of Recovery

For C.B. Miller, rehabilitation would play a big role in his comeback on both an inpatient and outpatient basis. As was always the case, the Millers did not make the decision to send their son there lightly. They visited and researched a number of rehab centers and cautiously check-marked the pluses and minuses of each.

The search started about a month after the accident, a time of great uncertainty tinged with hopefulness as C.B. seemed to be reawakening. Social services at Wilkes-Barre General made it clear that their part of the rehabilitation process was merely an initial step in C.B.'s comeback. He would have to be transferred to a rehabilitation facility eventually. There was time to do it, but how much time was unclear. All they knew came from the neurosurgeon, who said he wouldn't be moved until he was satisfied with his condition..

As it turned out, it would be another six or seven weeks before C.B. would need to move on. When they began researching their options for rehabilitation centers, Mike and Sharon weren't even sure just how much of C.B. would be left to resurrect. They agreed, however, that even as C.B. was struggling for consciousness, whatever obstacles they faced would not be treated as handicaps.

"We chose to treat obstacles as challenges," is how Mike, an admirer of the most famous advocate of positive thinking, Dr. Norman Vincent Peale, described their proactive approach. Handicaps you work around in benign acceptance. Challenges are something to be conquered.

You might think that such challenges would be daunting. Indeed, the Millers had little knowledge or expertise that would help them make this and many of the other decisions they would face in the last half of 1994. For Mike Miller, the research chemist, there was no mystery about what he had to do: Gather the information, learn and make an informed decision. Then do it all over again for the next challenge. What some might regard as another level of stress in dealing with a family tragedy, he regarded as a release, channeling his energy for the good of his son.

"We had a lot of learning to do," he said of his mindset at the time.

The chief informational source on traumatic brain injury in 1994 was the National Head Injury Foundation, which would later become the Brain Injury Association of America. The Internet was still in its early stages, and "Google" had yet to work its way into our vernacular. Information and resources couldn't be conjured up with a few strokes of the keyboard and a mouse click on the "search" button. Mike had to get information the old-fashioned way, querying by phone—the immobile kind anchored in homes and businesses. Then you waited for the literature to arrive by mail.

The basic information he received about brain injury recommended that they visit and interview three to five rehabilitation hospitals before making a decision. From there, following preliminary visits and interviews, you narrowed the field to the top two. Then you followed up with the favored two and the questions became more detailed, relating to the patient and his or her needs and how the services would be paid for. In a way, it was therapeutic, even empowering, for Mike Miller:

"This proved to be a very important process for us. Not only did it make us very aware of what the facility we chose could and would do for him, but it served as a mechanism for us to begin our learning process about the treatment of traumatic brain injury."

He learned the important questions that needed to be asked when they visited rehabilitation hospitals, including questions about the types of specialists they had on staff, what their priorities were in treating people with TBI, access to therapists and how the family was included in the process. It would be the family, after all, who would take over after the professionals did their thing.

No one could predict how C.B. would emerge from all of this. Would he be able to relearn even a fraction of what he needed to achieve even a semblance of independence? Would he be angry, sullen, prone to violence, unresponsive— all of which had been documented among people recovering from severe brain injury? During his visit to one of the rehabilitation hospitals, Mike Miller saw something that he thought no longer existed, the padded room. He couldn't help but picture C.B. in such a place.

"It made me imagine C.B. in a straitjacket or bouncing around in one of those rooms. The image made me sick to my stomach and filled me with fear for what he might have ahead of him."

The truth is that all the places they visited, even the one with the padded room, had strengths worth considering. Yet it was the John Heinz Institute of Rehabilitation and its staff that stood out. It also provided the extra benefit of being near C.B.'s college friends and two hours closer to the Millers' home than the second choice. Revisiting familiar places would be part of reintroducing their son to his old life in hopes of sparking a new one. It would be their job to do that.

What C.B. accomplished at Heinz was not much more than "a small step on a long road," Kopicki says. Progress was slow at first, but sparks were definitely igniting in C.B.'s impaired brain. One major accomplishment, in terms of communicating, took a month and a half to reach. C.B. uttered a three-word sentence: "I don't know."

"It was thrilling," says his father, who conceded that he and Sharon needed every positive morsel they could get during that period. The early days of his rehabilitation seemed the most tenuous. The shadow of doubt caused by the recent touch-and-go medical conditions lingered, at least in the subconscious, where worry often takes root. Yet there was hope, and everyone looked for continuing positive signs of what might predict his chances of making a full recovery.

While slow, the progress at Heinz was progress just the same, and every little gain meant a lot. And just when it seemed most encouraging, the Millers were to receive some unwelcome news from their insurance provider. After two months of intense rehab, C.B. was nearing the end of his allotted time for inpatient treatment at Heinz. His parents feared that taking him home at this time would be a major setback, possibly nullifying gains he had so laboriously achieved. They felt he needed more time before he was ready for outpatient rehab, but they were being told they couldn't get it.

It was a critical juncture in C.B.'s recovery and his family was up for the challenge.

CHAPTER 6

C.B. AS IN COMING BACK

C.B. was approaching the end of two months of inpatient rehabilitation at Heinz when word came that the insurers would no longer foot the bill. C.B. was to be discharged. This decision would subsequently be reversed. C.B. would get a substantial reprieve before being relegated to outpatient status. Had he not been given an extension of inpatient treatment, which came on the heels of two rejected appeals and getting an attorney involved, C.B. might not be regarded today as one of Heinz's star alumni.

"The longest we'd had anybody here was two months," Kopicki recalls, "and we were all surprised when the word came down that C.B. would be here for another two months." It had apparently been the insurance-covered standard for those with TBI: a maximum of two months of rehab before being transferred to a skilled nursing facility or, if their family could handle it, back to their homes. It wasn't a matter of being cut loose, left to fend for themselves. They would be eligible for daily outpatient rehabilitation, but that presented another barrier— the logistics and expense of getting the patient to and from their daily therapy sessions. For some TBI survivors, at the end of their financial tether and seeing little improvement, it could mean the end of their rehabilitation.

As for C.B., there was no chance of that— not with the relentless Mike and Sharon Miller behind him. His early recovery was a series of small victories, not dramatic triumphs. However, as he neared the end of those allotted two months, signs indicated that something extraordinary was in the making and keeping him there was critical. The story of how that was done comes later.

The individualized programs that Heinz created for C.B. called for four different distinct therapies: physical, occupational, speech and cognitive. At the time, this was standard for treating those with traumatic brain injury. Cognitive therapy deals with behavioral and emotional responses, which may be dramatically altered in the brain injured, resulting in dysfunctional thinking, anger issues, depression and passivity.

Intensive therapy in any and all of these areas can take its toll—even though respites are carefully built into the program. Stamina issues are common for people with TBI. The brain is healing, relearning and building bridges. That can be exhausting, even without the demands presented by the elements of therapy that require the patient to engage in physical exercises.

"This was a time of very hard work for him," Mike Miller recalls of the months at Heinz, "especially when you consider that he was inactive for three months prior to starting this work."

The hulking lineman who stepped out on that balcony had used up the physical advantage he had gained from his conditioning and youth. C.B. had been essentially bedridden while in the hospital, comatose much of that time. He came to Heinz almost as helpless as an infant—a very large infant. He had to relearn how to walk, talk and perform the most basic functions, daily activities most of us take for granted. In another sense, he was old before his time due to the wear, tear and toll the injuries had taken on his body and brain. The right side of his body, even with a best-case rehabilitation outcome, would never function properly and they would discover he was deaf in his left ear.

As a result of his injuries, C.B. suffered from expressive aphasia, a language disorder. People with this disorder know what they want to say but have troubles finding the words they need to express themselves. Because of the aphasia, therapists were still not sure what remained of C.B.'s brain in terms of thought patterns, recognition and basic vocabulary. While much of his recovery is a foggy memory, C.B. does remember the frustration of not being able to get the words out.

During their regular evening visits, C.B.'s parents were encouraged by the therapists to engage him in more exercises if possible. It became clear to them, however, that C.B. was physically and mentally spent by that time of the day.

"The best we could do was to play the simple card games that he remembered and help him to relax," his father explains. When he did respond appropriately to these simple diversions, they were thrilled. They would end those visits on a high and animatedly discuss the successes on the long drive home.

During weekends, when C.B. underwent little or no therapy, his parents felt they had their greatest impact. They decided it would be therapeutic to get him out of the rehabilitation center, especially with him more rested and seemingly energized by the change in scenery and daily therapy schedule. After training from the staff on how to transfer C.B. in and out of their vehicle, they would take him on short drives. They found all kinds of places to take him in hopes of continuing to challenge his healing brain. Their expectations grew in direct proportion to their growing confidence in handling C.B. and his own receptiveness.

"At first we would simply take him out for a fifteen- to twenty-minute drive from the rehab hospital," says Mike, noting that this was all C.B. could tolerate at first. The trick was to take him to places with which he was familiar, such as the Wilkes University campus, the resort where he worked and his previous haunts in Wilkes-Barre.

"You could tell he enjoyed the excursions," his father said. The outings became longer, and they would often park on campus, transfer him into his wheelchair and take him to his old dorm and other hangouts. "Because of his expressive aphasia he could not tell us how he felt, but he could get a lot across just by expressions."

Even with the words trapped inside, C.B. had been quite expressive from the start of his stay at Heinz. He expressed himself through physical responses or a knowing look in his eyes. These subtle cues spoke volumes to C.B.'s family and friends. And his parents became increasingly optimistic that the personality that emerged would not be that of a stranger. Their belief that his comeback would be something special, no matter how sluggish it seemed at times, was buoyed by their times with him. As often as not, the greatest triumphs during that period came at the most unexpected times.

On one of their weekend excursions, Mike and Sharon took C.B. to the college cafeteria, where he was known by most of the students. The story of his accident and survival had been in the news from the start. Students immediately welcomed C.B. and engaged with him. The give and take from social interaction in such settings, even with C.B. being essentially unresponsive verbally, was clearly good for him. Something was happening in that brain of his.

During that cafeteria visit, a tall young man sauntered into the cafeteria wearing a hat. He grabbed the attention of C.B., who became animated and began pointing at the hat. C.B. obviously recognized the young fellow and seemed to want his parents to know that. After speaking to the young man, they learned that C.B. had given the hat to him prior to his accident, and they are thrilled at this display of memory, evidence that he could bring the past and the present together. This would be critical if he were to move ahead with anything approaching a normal life.

"Although C.B. could not tell us the story himself," as his father put it, "just the evidence that he had the memory was very exciting to us."

Were one to think of these horrible injuries as an ongoing tragedy, as some parents might, the incident in the cafeteria could have been disheartening, not uplifting. A young man unable to share a simple story, other than excitedly gesture and point at a hat, might be seen as a reminder of how far he had fallen. For Mike and Sharon Miller, it was a milestone to be treasured and, as it turned out, undeniable proof that their son was on the mend.

Of course, C.B. had his own stories, thoughts he could not share with anyone at that time. They were all in there, and he was coming to his first realizations that his life would never be the same. This was the only time after the accident, he concedes today, in which he was angry with God and perhaps feeling a little sorry for himself. The aphasia made it worse, leaving him incapable of expressing his thoughts or sharing his doubts with someone who might help him process them. He was left mostly to deal with those on his own. Yet all was not lost. The unabated optimism of his parents kept him on a steady climb, even if the ascent seemed negligible at times.

He did have a girlfriend when the accident happened, but she didn't stick around. It was not serious enough to take her home to meet the folks, but she was his main squeeze, as they said back in the 1990's when he was going to college. He is not bitter about it—quite understanding, in fact— and he has only seen her once since, at a Wilkes Homecoming. She gave him a sisterly kiss and he was fine with that. It is one of those nice memories of his previous life, much like his continued fondness for boyhood and college friends.

At this early stage of his recovery, C.B. understood that everyone in it with him at that point would be in it for the long haul: "There was a pretty good chance I'd never be self-sufficient, and that's a lot to ask of a person, staying with you when you got something like that ahead of you."

Getting Past the Pain for Life Changing Gains...

When C.B. was dealing with the loss and harboring some resentment, there were moments when he might not have worked as diligently at his therapy as he should have. One of his therapists reported that he was not trying very hard and, ultimately, refused to come to a scheduled session. This had the potential of derailing his rehab. She subsequently offered the professional opinion that the pain was the intimidator, notably pain experienced during the dexterity therapy on his right arm, which had been rendered almost useless by his brain injury. C.B. insists in retrospect that it was about communication. Make that no communication. Because he was nonverbal, the therapist worked in silence. He was accustomed to being talked to, verbally encouraged. The approach left him feeling totally unmotivated, but he was unable at the time to let anyone know what the problem was.

His brother happened to be at Heinz during this low point—perhaps the lowest since he was wheeled into the emergency room more than three months before. "He told me that if I was not willing to do the work I was going to be a vegetable the rest of my life. It was like he said to me 'You've got a choice: Do this and get along with your life or die.' I decided I did not want to die."

Today, C.B. is fond of telling his audiences about this get-off-your-butt-or-die ultimatum. His brother does not remember making such a blunt assessment, but it is obviously very real to C.B. It is so real that it became a motivational mantra. He shares it years later with a classroom of adolescent boys who have all been kicked out of their public schools as essentially incorrigible. They are in a program of last resort, fulfilling the state-mandated requirement for attending school until the age of sixteen. The system regards them as expendable, lost causes, and C.B. is there to motivate them. Indeed, his account does seem to impress them, and their speaker is a flesh-and-blood example of the seeming unfairness of life, and that you've got to make the most of what you've got.

"A lot of people give up, and not just brain injured people," C.B. tells them. "I'm a fighter, and you've got a lot more going for you than I did then."

His recovery during therapy was hard work. It was painful and fatiguing, both physically and mentally, and the two months he was assured for inpatient rehab were nearing their end as the Thanksgiving holiday approached in 1994. As for the process of reclaiming his speech, he had barely put a dent in that. His vocabulary was pretty much restricted to "yes" and "no."

If he needed more inspiration, he got it from Don Mosley, his roommate at Heinz. Mosley had sustained his traumatic brain injuries in an accident in Colorado while a cadet at the U.S. Air Force Academy. His best friend was killed in the same accident and Mosley's survival, like C.B.'s, was attributed to his youth and his superb physical condition.

"Don always said 'Pain is temporary; pride is forever,'" says C.B. of the former Division I college basketball player who shared his room at Heinz. "I still use that phrase today. It's true. You've got to overcome obstacles."

And yet even Mosley would confess several years later in a TBI chat room that he often felt sorry for himself as he recovered from the injuries that diverted him from a promising military career. Not only did his future seem bleak, but he found himself contemplating suicide.

Apparently Mosley could at least express his feelings when he came to Heinz, which was C.B.'s most frustrating barrier.

From the beginning, music seemed to open some kind of communication channel. C.B. likes his music, and the first time he remembers really starting to say something is when it came out through singing. The song was one that had been popular a couple of years before his accident— "Ice Ice Baby" by Vanilla Ice. He's not sure what part of the hip hop classic came out, but it probably wasn't the lyric: "I'm killin' your brain like a poisonous mushroom..."

As was the case when he started singing "Three Times a Lady" when quizzed by his sister about the 3:33 on the digital clock, music allowed him to pull out certain words or concepts. He also recalls humming the melodies of songs at Heinz when he really could not express himself otherwise vocally. It makes sense, because it is generally held that music and other creative skills come from the brain's right cerebral cortex while fundamental word skills originate in the left— the side almost obliterated in C.B.'s fall. To this day, he still struggles to read and write, which makes him technically illiterate.

For the most part, Sharon Miller never left her son's side until he took up residency at the John Heinz Institute of Rehabilitation in Wilkes-Barre. It was almost three months — essentially the summer of 1994— before a day passed without them seeing each other. And she still managed to make the trip to Heinz at least a couple of evenings a week and on weekends over the span of four months of inpatient rehabilitation. She was the one who kept the closest tabs on him, continuing the journal she had started during the dark days at the hospital.

The day following their first one apart since the July 21st accident, October 15, she was there when C.B. took his first shower. She was delighted when, as he parted company with his clothes, he announced,

"Shoes off!" It may not be a grammatically correct sentence, but it was a complete thought expressed verbally.

By the way, most patients don't go to bed with their shoes on, but while in the hospital C.B. was the exception. He wore his big sneakers in bed to keep his right foot, affected by his brain injury, from drooping. The sight of C.B, in bed, with those big sneakers sticking up in the air, certainly elicited double takes from visitors and staffers passing by.

A few days later, his roommate, Mosley, confided in Sharon that C.B had been grousing because when his parents visit in the evening they immediately try to force him to eat, as well as nag him about doing exercises recommended by his therapists. As his father would later realize, C.B. was pretty much wiped out from a full day of therapy by the time they got there.

"He [Don Mosley] made me realize that we were not giving you enough space," his mother related in a journal entry directed to her son.

October 22 was a red-letter day for 21-year-old C.B. On the three-month anniversary of his fall, they took him to a Wilkes football game to cheer on the team on which he had expected to play. It was a milestone occasion in a number of ways. For starters, he smiled for the first time, possibly sensing, at last, that some kind of normal life awaited him. He watched the action from a wheelchair, asking only for something to support his damaged right arm. A tray pulled out of the trunk of their car served that purpose. Despite his obvious excitement over being there, he only had the stamina to make it until halftime.

By the end of October, his distinctive laugh had returned and he was trying very hard to talk. Although the words weren't exactly tumbling out after a month at Heinz, he was clearly much more alert and focused. His parents were convinced more than ever that C.B. would conquer the aphasia if they continued to work him as hard as they had.

A few weeks after his first visit, C.B. returned to Ralston Field— this time to attend the homecoming game. His whole family, including siblings, accompanied him to the event. He was guest of honor— "Colonel of the Week" and honorary co-captain— at a home game with rival Kings College. A photo of him in a wheelchair appeared in the Citizen's Voice newspaper. A jacket draped over his injured right shoulder and arm, and C.B. holding his left hand over his damaged left eye. Later he'll be outfitted with an eye patch, making him look like a baby-faced pirate. Coach DeMelfi talked to his former talkative lineman, now silenced by aphasia, and Sharon Miller observed that the coach is "somewhat emotional."

C.B. sat in his chair atop an embankment overlooking the field, there "by the grace of God and sheer will of a lion," according to a newspaper account of the special day. Indeed, he was there with a severely damaged brain, a rearranged face, repaired broken upper and lower jaws and a broken wrist. No football player on the field had to work harder, sacrifice more, to be at that game.

C.B. still goes to the Homecoming games and always gets the royal treatment

Following that day, Phil Gianficaro's sports column in the Citizen's Voice was headlined "C.B. as in Coming Back. " When it was read to him, C.B. betrayed obvious emotion. "You nearly cried a couple of times and, of course, I did cry," his mother wrote to him in her journal. "This is the most emotion we have seen since the accident. You are coming back more each day!"

Noteworthy November

It is November, and C.B. seems more active verbally. He doesn't say much, but one of the things he says the most is, "Oh, shit!" He is apparently into exclamatory remarks, because his other favorite saying is, "Holy cow!" When asked if his dad could get out the clippers and give him a haircut, C.B. responds by saying, "I think not."

All of these remarks, no matter how simple or basic, represent significant gains. His vocabulary, however, remains limited to a handful of words. At this juncture, his actions literally speak louder than words. When his mother volunteers to take home and wash the sweat pants he wears almost continually, he surprises her by taking them off and handing them to her. Obviously, the occupational therapy, relearning basic tasks, is working.

Another reason to be encouraged is that he is speaking reactively, responding to a comment or sentence by completing a thought or with a logical reply. When his Dad says, "We are...," C.B. says, "Penn State!" When one of his parents says, "Thank you," he says, "You're welcome!"

Even though he hasn't reached the point where he can express his feelings or make subjective observations, the small victories continue. When asked if he wants his hair cut he shouts, "Help, Help!" and laughs. He takes to saying, "Well, I oughta" a lot, but what he oughta do is apparently a mystery, even to himself. When he is told on November 15 that his parents are going on a business trip but won't be back for a number of days, he gives them an impish grin and says, "Nuts." Sister, Kathie, asks him about his roommate on the phone, and C.B. observes, "He's a character." When his father walks into his room without a coat on Dec. 4, C.B. asks, "Is it that hot?" When he leaves to get rid of some trash, C.B. quips, "Take your time."

Sometimes, there is a hint of a vocabulary in there somewhere. When a neighbor, Fred Place, starts to leave after a visit, C.B. says, "I'm appreciative." Even twenty years after the accident, he surprises himself when some words pop out.

One night just before Thanksgiving, C.B. greets everyone by humming the Budweiser beer song of the time, continuing to hum it all evening.

So Much to Be Thankful for…

It is Thanksgiving, November 24th, and C.B. is coming home to Towanda. It is only for the day, but it is a major milestone in his recovery. Along the way, signs and banners welcome him home, with a three-mile stretch in neighboring Wysox displaying an impressive array of messages. A huge banner at the end of the river bridge entering Towanda welcomes him home, as does the marquee of the historic Keystone Theatre on his hometown's Main Street. C.B. is clearly moved by the attention and the communal compassion.

It has been four months and three days since the fall.

As soon as he arrives home, he flashes a triumphant thumb's up. His first words comprise one of the lengthiest sentences he has uttered to date: "I have to go to the bathroom." He had been desperate to attend to that need for much of the ride home, but the logistics and dearth of appropriate facilities along the route made it impossible.

Being back home is like a shot in the arm—a reminder that all the hard work had been worth it. C.B. settles in the TV room, dining on cottage cheese as his chief solid food. Sharon still has to administer tube feedings. In the meantime, many people stop to visit and wish him well. He regularly walks around with assistance, as if making the point that he will soon be able to fend for himself. At the end of his stay, he insists on walking with an assist to the car instead of relying on the wheelchair.

In December they start bringing him home just for the day on weekends. Things seem to be moving quickly, and nobody is more excited than C.B. He happily tells Kathie on the phone on the 13th, "Tube out yesterday," referring to the fact that they'd removed his feeding tube.

He gets to place the first ornament on Christmas tree when he comes home for the day on December 17th. The entire family celebrates Christmas early on Sunday, the 18th, so everyone could be there. Like a little kid when opening gifts, CB seems stuck on three words, "Wow, oh wow!" He goes to church at St. Peter and Paul's for first time since the accident, still grateful for the congregation's support and especially impressed that they held a special mass for him after his accident. He believes this has made a difference in his recovery. Prayers and positive thinking have always been esteemed in the Miller household.

Upon returning to his home away from home, he tells therapist, "I had a fantastic time." Complete sentences are more frequent now, and subjective opinions and qualitative judgments are emerging. As if putting an exclamation point on a joyous holiday weekend with his family, he breaks into a dance and does a hip bump with Kathie at Heinz.

On the day of Christmas Eve, his parents take him to Wilkes-Barre General Hospital to visit those who treated him and delivered him from death's doorstep. He has only murky memories of this place. Most of what he knows happened here was conveyed to him by his parents and others, but he knows they saved his life. As he is wheeled around the hospital, he gets out of his wheelchair to hug staffers. They present him with a pillow. "It's a nice surprise," he tells them. Later they also pay a visit to Dean Jane Lampe-Groh at her Wilkes-Barre residence, and CB looks around, impressed. "It's marvelous," he says.

"Merry Christmas" and "Happy New Year" are constant refrains on Christmas Day 1994 when C.B. greets his family at Heinz. Later, upon being returned to the hospital, he motions his mother and sister, Kathie, toward him with his good arm. "A family hug," he tells them as they embrace.

He is becoming increasingly independent, putting on and taking off his clothes, as the end of the year approaches. Before going home for the New Year's weekend, he entertains the nurses at the station. "He's a comic," one of them observes amid the laughter.

At home he is very active and kidding around when cousins come to visit. He is ringing out the old year on a high note. He negotiates the stairs, up and down, with one bad leg and one bad arm. It is a testament, if not symbolic, to how far he had come

C.B. visits Heinz often nowadays, and the staff there treats him like an old friend, even though some twenty years have passed since he was a patient there. In many ways, his months at Heinz were both frustrating and painful, but to him it's like a second home. He was accepted as part of a family there, and now he is one of their stars. He has lost some friends and associates elsewhere—some because life tends to separate people as the years go by and, in C.B.'s case, traumatic brain injury does change the chemistry in your relationships with old friends. You're not quite the same. Everybody else is well into a career, raising families and dealing with being middle-aged. C.B., however, is 40 going on 18. He belongs to a demographic called TBI and though it is both exclusive and confining, there are some 5.3 million others in the same fold. That's comparable to the populations of Atlanta and Miami.

At Heinz, time seems to stand still when he returns there, as he does quite often to this day. Altough a number of people who worked with him are no longer there, some of the old gang, like Kopicki, remain, and others have come to know him from his frequent visits. Those who remain have become good friends. Kopicki, for instance, invited C.B. to her daughter's graduation as one of an intimate group of family and friends.

"You've come a long way, baby!" exults one Heinz staffer named Colleen, when she sees C.B. in the cafeteria during one visit. It seems that everyone who knows him sees him as a success story, as someone who has exceeded expectations. Others see him as someone who is disabled, something of a colorful character on the perimeter of their busy lives.

CHAPTER 7

REFUSING TO SET LIMITS

Mike Miller was a research chemist, with the emphasis on research. He is the type of guy who believes there are answers for everything. All you have to do is find them. They may emerge from a conversation or an interview. There may be a study out there that will open a door, even if just a crack, and, in the age of the internet, the people with the answers and the information are much more accessible. The trick is to not be overwhelmed, to know what to throw away and what to keep.

His relentless mindset became a powerful tool. If the answer, or even a clue to the answer, is out there, he will relentlessly track it down. If this were a war of survival, which is how Mike Miller approached it, that relentlessness might be called a weapon. That is especially true in describing his approach to dealing with the traumatic brain injury of his youngest son, C.B. It is essentially about being proactive, Miller will tell you. It's about taking the initiative when you confront an obstacle, and though now in his seventies and as proactive as ever, he believes that being told no or that you can't do something is often the beginning, not the end, of the process.

Miller is the ultimate go-to guy. He knows how to get things done, whether it is organizing a state Little League tournament in his small town, or leading the effort to spearhead the passage of a high school sports concussion bill by the Pennsylvania legislature and subsequently signed by the governor, as Miller was able to do in November of 2011. His experience with C.B. and TBI led him to the Pennsylvania Brain Injury Coalition, comprised of a number of associations and organizations working cooperatively on state legislative issues on behalf of the brain injured. He currently chairs the coalition, with an abiding interest in protecting high school athletes from perils posed by concussions and how scholastic sports programs may most effectively respond to this health threat. The bill, which took effect throughout the state in June of 2012, floundered the first time Miller, at the helm of the coalition, worked with his organization to get it through. It was just another rejection that would ultimately be overcome. The way he looks at it, sometimes you need to be rebuffed to get their attention.

He is at the forefront of brain injury and concussion issues. Yet you wouldn't know it because he seems to be off to the side in the photos, maybe partially obstructed in the back row. He's never out front taking the bows. His efforts with Little League, his church, raising money for community endeavors, at the same time learning and advancing in his career, attest to his compulsion to make things better for his family and community. It is self-improvement at its purest, but Mike Miller is not a self promoter.

"I challenge you to find something my Dad hasn't mastered," says son, Michael. "He is the master organizer, learning facilitator… That guy understands how to get the most out of people. That guy knows how to optimize people around him."

In appearance, he's just an average guy. Average height, average build with a few extra pounds to lose, though he is in better shape than most guys his age. He works at staying in shape, physically and mentally. If you drew a caricature of him you'd play up the thick glasses and round face, but his quick smile puts you at ease right away. He enjoys his friends and their banter when they meet regularly in the morning at a restaurant, the Weigh Station, for coffee and to solve the world's problems. Mike listens, and with his laughter and obvious enjoyment of their company encourages the discourse of his band of brothers, most of them retired and ranging in age from their sixties to their eighties.

Mike Miller relishes the fundamental things of life, and he really loves sports. It is one reason he chose stemming the damage of concussions among high school athletes as a cause. His efforts to learn more about brain injury led him to the Brain Injury Association of America, then known as the National Head Injury Foundation, and subsequently to the Pennsylvania association where his most recent role has been as vice president. But it was his love of high school and collegiate sports, plus seeing young athletes whose lives have been irreparably harmed by failures in properly treating concussions, that turned him into an activist dedicated to doing something about this most common type of brain injury.

He has been a radio commentator for years covering high school football and basketball, mostly with a long-time friend, Milt Munkittrick. In fact, if you say "Milt and Mike" in Towanda, or in Bradford County for that matter, most automatically know who you are talking about. More recently, Mike has been teaming on the radio with a younger partner and former sports editor, Bob Baker, in covering teams from north-central Pennsylvania, as well as southern

New York. All of them are essentially rural school districts with a small town at their hubs.

Then there is the Mllers' favorite college team. Two of their children, Michael and Kathie, are Penn State alumni, and the Miller family makes regular pilgrimages to University Park on Saturdays in the fall to tailgate and cheer on the Nittany Lions at Beaver Stadium. Even Sharon, converted out of necessity, is an avid Penn State fan and has learned to talk the talk with the most informed of the followers.

"I really wasn't that much into football," Sharon confesses. "I learned that either you sit and sulk or you join them. I enjoy the games now."

The Penn State excursions also provide occasional reunions with son, Michael, who joins them at some of the home games. They remain true blue— Penn State blue, that is—even in their recent fall from grace in the wake of the Jerry Sandusky criminal case. A breast cancer diagnosis for Sharon and subsequent aggressive treatment through chemo and radiation therapy altered the course of their lives in the summer and fall of 2012, but they proceed without complaint and a positive approach that Mike Miller's guru, the late Norman Vincent Peale, would surely find inspiring.

C.B. used to go to Penn State games occasionally, but now he most often chooses to stay home. The crowd noise and cold wind blowing into his damaged and dry left eye, make the experience something of an ordeal for him. He likes the tailgating part and the abundance of food his mom brings along. The brain injury has taken away his sense of taste, but C.B. still enjoys eating. He remembers how food tasted before his accident, and when he's eating a cheeseburger, for instance, what he is experiencing is the vivid memory of how a cheeseburger tastes. His memory, in fact, has been his salvation, and since his learning process is oral, memory is the key.

What is memory? How much is overt and how much in the subconscious? C.B. has no conscious memories of all those weeks in the hospital. He was actually being stood up and walked around, responding nonverbally, even monosyllabically, but none of that is remembered. Could the subconscious—what happened there, what he heard there— contribute to his sense of well-being and the positive way he has dealt with his brain injury since the early days of his therapy?

There is no question in Mike Miller's mind that the course for C.B.'s comeback was set in motion when he was seemingly unresponsive and uncomprehending. Brain science backs him up in that belief, though mystery still shrouds just what does and doesn't impact the brain in a comatose or semiconscious state. Learning can apparently take place in the subconscious, even without explicit memory to support it.

Even when C.B. was in a coma, unresponsive, his father understood that his son should be talked to, read to, touched and even included in conversations around his bedside. Shortly after the accident, their parish priest at the time set the course for this approach. The clergyman, as the victim of a house fire, had himself been in a coma, offering some insight that the Millers would take to heart. The priest recalled the frustration of being comatose and hearing people talk about him as if he weren't there. His advice was to assume C.B., even with his brain, the engine, barely idling, would be influenced, perhaps unconsciously, by what was being said in his presence.

Great Comebacks Start with Defying Convention…

The decision Mike Miller made to keep C.B. engaged and encouraged from the start was the first of many decisions that would make C.B.'s comeback as complete as possible. The goal was to give him the tools he would need to be independent and, perhaps more importantly, restore a quality of life, even if it wouldn't be the same as that of his previous life. At that point, they didn't know if the person emerging from the coma would even resemble the old C.B.

"You need to understand the circumstances as much as you can, make a decision and then don't second-guess that decision," Mike says. "You can't be an expert in everything. You just can't."

The game plan that evolved clashed with the conventional treatment of traumatic brain injury at the time, which imposed limits on what could be regained in the healing and therapy that comes in the aftermath of TBI. It also collided with the kid-gloves approach that failure was something to be avoided in the recovery process. Mike was to come to the conclusion through his research and resources, that there should be no time limit, no cut-off point, on regaining brain functions. It was the person-controlled model eventually agreed upon, which revolved around the following maxim:

"Let them try what they want to do, and be there for them in case they fail."

Indeed, the conventional approach has been revised somewhat, substantiating that the strategy with C.B. was more effective than the one espoused by the experts in the mid-1990's. Now brain scientists are saying that the most significant improvements to so-called cognitive deficits take place within the two years following the injury, with the most dramatic occurring over the first six months. They don't rule out gradual improvements after those two years. Mike Miller might not agree with that entirely, based on C.B.'s continuing recovery over almost two decades. Whatever the parameters imposed by the so-called experts, C.B. Miller, the patient, continues to evolve and the comeback is never truly complete.

"One of the first things you have to recognize is that you are your own advocate," is another of Mike's mantras. He took his lead from the late Christopher Reeve, who played Superman on film but was genuinely heroic in the years after a fall from a horse resulted in him becoming a quadriplegic. Reeve made the point that only about 30 percent of people seriously impaired by injury or illness appeal after their insurance claims are rejected.

"You don't ever accept a rejection," Miller learned from the actor and activist, who he, C.B., Sharon and daughter, Kathie, got to hear speak several years before his death in 2004. "Always appeal."

The seed for this approach may have been planted by the doctor in the Miller family when he refused to accept the original neurosurgeon's wait-and-see stance as his brother hovered close to death. Never accept rejection. In this instance it was the launching of the progressive approach that would subsequently become the hallmark of C.B.'s comeback. The noncommittal neurosurgeon was essentially rejected in favor of one who viewed his patient as one with a future beyond mere survival.

Once C.B. had progressed beyond survival mode, it was important to recognize the tools that were still at his command and the ones that weren't. During the first year or so of his long rehabilitation process, it was about retrieving as much of what had been lost as possible.

The prospect of furthering his education, let alone continuing college studies, would have seemed far-fetched then. They were to learn that C.B.'s keen memory and hard work, teamed with software allowing him to learn orally on his own, would open doors that would have never been imagined when C.B. was at Heinz, still struggling to get the words out.

C.B. reaffirmed his father's belief that if you keep trying, amazing things may happen. There was something else learned by Mike Miller, a man of boundless energy and many friends who gave so much to his church and community. There was a reservoir of people out there, all willing to help with whatever they could contribute, that would greatly ease the burden of the journey ahead.

"We kept trying things and people always seemed to be willing to do it," is the way he describes it. "Every one of them had a positive impact."

People power, the willingness of others to help, was evident from the early days after C.B.'s accident, starting when Mike and Sharon returned home to find a group of friends mowing and trimming their lawn. But that was only a sampling of the effort that was to come after C.B. returned home, still missing the basic tools needed to get on with his life. It seemed that all Mike Miller had to do was ask and he received. He talked to the director of a two-county literacy program, which relied on volunteer tutors to help adults learn to read and write, and two Towanda women, Mary Alice Demangone and Barbara Ulatowski, stepped forward to tutor C.B.

Mike's brother, J. Ed, suggested that C.B. would benefit from an association with Serve, Inc., a workshop and counseling agency for the disabled, and he got his first job through them, taking photo IDs for Pennsylvania driver's licenses at a local testing center. This presented a daily opportunity to interact with a variety of people and to flex the social skills that were quite rudimentary at the time. C.B., whose humor isn't always taken as such by those who don't know him, also learned that there are certain nuances required in social interaction. A humorous aside, for instance, may be taken as threatening or suggestive, especially coming from a big man with a deadpan delivery.

Then there would be the commitment of Sylvia Abrams, former teacher and mother of one of C.B.'s high school classmates, whose coaching and skills as a reading specialist increased his vocabulary exponentially, as well as his effectiveness as a motivational speaker.

Looking at all the volunteer hours that were so generously given to assist in C.B.'s comeback, it is no wonder that Mike and Sharon Miller were joyful at a party celebrating their youngest son's graduation from college sixteen years after his accident. The process of earning a bachelor's degree itself took eleven years. That came after the monitoring of high school classes, the tutoring and the ongoing instruction from Abrams and others.

About 200 people attended the celebration at the Catholic community center in Towanda, all of whom had played a role in C.B.'s comeback, and it was as much a way of thanking the community as it was lauding his accomplishment. It had been constructed one course at a time at a college satellite office, with the mortar being many hours of study to reinforce the lessons in the classroom.

But perhaps the most impressive display of friendship and volunteerism, in terms of people involved and hours committed, came when C.B. completed four months of inpatient rehab at Heinz and needed to return on an outpatient basis in the early months of 1995, commuting from home every day.

With time running out on C.B.'s inpatient status at Heinz, Mike and Sharon Miller knew that the next step, bringing him home and then conveying him back and forth for outpatient rehabilitation, was not only necessary but critical. Sharon was willing to give up her work and be with C.B. all the time, which would include taxiing him daily on the three-hour round trip. However, both were well aware that this would mean her day-to-day existence would totally hinge on C.B.'s ups and downs.

It was a lesson they had learned from those months in the hospital and then at Heinz: "From our prior experience we knew that if either of us spends all of our time with C. B. our only good days will be his good days and visa versa," Mike reasoned.

"You won't be there to pick each other up," warned son, Michael, who was the first to discourage them from making C.B.'s continued rehabilitation a full-time thing.

With barely a month to go before the rehab would have to continue on an outpatient basis, they knew they had to have a plan. At the same time, they were hoping there was a way for both of them to continue their jobs and some semblance of a normal life. They still had to be there for their son evenings and weekends and needed all the energy and enthusiasm they could muster. There were civil liability actions initiated at this time based on what appeared to be a strong case against the landlord. Yet there was still uncertainty about what services would continue to be provided to C.B. at this time and whether intense rehabilitation would continue to be extended based on the merits of their case.

There was a lot to be stressed out about as they entered February of 1995, almost seven months after the fall.

Getting By with Some Help from their Friends...

Their many good friends and church family turned out to be the solution to their greatest concern— getting C.B. to and from his sessions at Heinz seventy miles away while getting back to as normal a routine as possible with a brain injured son to nurture and motivate. They learned that some had already taken the ball and started it rolling. That ball, like one on a downhill slope, had gained momentum with amazing results. A trio of friends— Ed Branish, Monte Hughey and John Demangone—had come up with a plan to get C.B. to and from rehab every day with a network of volunteer drivers. That would mean each volunteer would give up that day—multiple days in many cases—to get C.B. to and from Wilkes-Barre. What they did prior to the return trip in the late afternoon would be up to them.

It was a logistical masterpiece and, before it was over, more that a hundred different people in their small town got involved in this operation. On Fridays, one of the organizers would drop off a calendar at the Millers with the names of the volunteers who would be driving the next week. Everything was good to go, and all Mike had to do the evening before was call the next day's scheduled driver to confirm.

On the eighth day of February, after four months at Heinz, C.B., exuberantly yelling, "Woo, woo, woo!" at the prospect of going home to stay, rode away from the rehab facility with his parents. Of course, he would still spend more of his waking hours away from home during the week—either on the road or at Heinz—but it was clearly a psychological lift for the entire family. With it came the peace of mind that on Feb. 13, his first day as an outpatient, there would be someone to provide the transportation for what turned out to be many months of vital rehabilitation.

The drivers were volunteers, but they also took the step of hiring a home health nurse to accompany C.B., each day. His vocabulary remained very limited, and he was still a big man at well over 200 pounds. The combination of those two factors, Mike suspected, might be intimidating for the volunteers, alone with him for three hours in a car, not knowing his son that well. It was a great way to launch the operation, because the nurse and C.B. got along exceedingly well, becoming, in Mike's words, "a great pair."

There were huge gains in that first month of outpatient therapy, and being home may have been a big reason for that. Stir in the interaction with the nurse, Linda VanDeWeert, and various volunteer drivers each day, and the recipe for a comeback seemed hopeful indeed. In fact, his communication skills and cognitive abilities had improved so dramatically by mid-March that the nurse agreed she was no longer needed on the trips. Indeed, C.B. Miller never seemed to tire of meeting new people and launching new friendships.

Brain injury survivors are known to sometimes act out aggressively or become sullen or angry. This never happened with C.B., something that Mike and Sharon, in retrospect, regarded as another blessing.

The pool of volunteers never dried up, meaning that this operation could continue indefinitely.

"This was beneficial to us in a lot of ways. It allowed us to be somewhat rested in the evening to help C.B.," Mike explains. "For example, I would read to him after dinner and show him the words as I read. In addition to this I could pursue ideas that we could use with C.B. after his outpatient therapy was complete. As the year progressed, his actual therapy days reduced from five to three. He would volunteer at John Heinz on some of his off days and the volunteers, recognizing the benefit to him, still drove him on those days."

Nobody is more thankful for all those volunteer drivers than C.B. himself: "There were something like 100 people on call ... It's amazing, truly amazing."

In many ways, people stepping up to volunteer was the Millers' best resource. It freed Mike so he could continue to work, spend quality time with C.B. and deal with a host of legal and financial measures that needed to be in place if C.B. was to become independent. Even today, with all the amazing gains, Mike is looking for continued improvement. Indeed C.B. proved he could do more and more on his own, including sustained periods in the spring of 2012 where his parents were away for weeks at a time dealing with his mother's breast cancer issues. C.B. lived up to all expectations.

That doesn't mean they don't continue to worry about him. They don't have the luxury of being content about where he is now. Both Mike and Sharon are committed to making sure he continues to move forward, at the same time enjoying what he has accomplished so far. "Enjoy," as you'll see, is one of C.B.'s favorite words.

"We're just going to keep moving, and when the good Lord's ready we'll go ahead and make changes as needed," says Mike, who with Sharon's illness and treatment seems even more keenly aware that his son needs to be prepared to make it on his own. "The important thing is we're still seeing growth and it's a question of continuing to grow."

C.B. still has the mindset of the athlete he used to be. He tends to think more in terms of conquering, overcoming obstacles, rather than growing. He realizes that, in the eyes of many, he is seen as "a question mark," a work in progress. Yet he and his father are basically on the same page on this point.

"You've got to push on," C.B. says of his continuing recovery. "You've got to survive and move on."

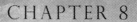

CHAPTER 8

"WHAT I NEEDED WERE SOME NUNS"

When you talk to C.B. Miller, whether in person or on the phone, he'll usually sign off with a single parting word, "Enjoy." That one word tells you pretty much all you need to know about him. That's what he does with his life—He enjoys it. More importantly, he continues to heal and grow, even 20 years after the accident. He also continues to astound.

"When I wake up every day, I enjoy myself," CB says. He adds that "enjoy" is one of his mantras.

"I'm a lucky, lucky man," he'll often say when he looks back on the adventure of what he calls his second life, even the parts that weren't exactly his shining moments. He accepts them all, but he is most pleased with the life he has built for himself.

If there were ever anyone who truly appreciates what he has, it is C.B. Miller. There seems to be no sense of loss. No anger or indignation ever emerges. Memories of who he was, the promise of his life before, are like treasures he can pick up, dust off and examine whenever he wishes. Even the food he can't taste, injected by the flavors from his memory, becomes something that he relishes. He is as fascinated by the missteps of his previous life as he is by his successes in his current one.

Here's someone who was in a coma for the better part of two months. He required a host of major surgeries and a battery of specialists and surgeons, followed by interminable months of demanding therapies just to begin his life again. After regaining consciousness, most of the words he wanted to communicate seemed trapped inside his head, unable to find their way to his lips. They were like phantoms, hovering nearby but never quite in reach. That's one effect traumatic brain injury can have on the brain, especially in cases where injuries are as severe as C.B.'s were. Expressive aphasia means not being able to communicate how you feel or find the words you want to say. The frustration must have been overwhelming.

The aphasia was never completely conquered, but C.B. understands that, even cheerfully acknowledges it. Understanding and acknowledging the aphasia is not the same as accepting it, because he's determined to keep progressing. No limits, as the slogan goes.

"The brain is a work in progress, and the progress can be lifelong," says Dr. Ellen McHugh, an M.D. and specialist in pediatric medicine at the Upstate Medical Center in Syracuse, NY. She is an expert on the brain and how it decodes words for reading and speaking. C.B. Miller, in his second life, believes he will continue to progress with his vocabulary, even though reading skills remain primitive.

C.B. has lived nearly half his life since the accident, which he considers to be the beginning of his life. In that way at least, he is not a man who's rapidly approaching middle age, but an adolescent, still exploring and, yes, enjoying.

"I was 21 when it happened," he says matter-of-factly a few weeks before his 39th birthday in May of 2012. "In, what, three years I'll have lived longer after the accident than before it…" By this reckoning, in his second life he has not yet reached the age of his previous one. C.B. possesses the maturity and calm of an old soul. At the same time, he is childlike. When talking about a number of family members who have passed on, including a favorite uncle and both his grandmothers, he says plaintively, "I hope I'm gonna go to heaven and talk to my family."

The C.B. Miller who leaned against that railing could be both saintly and cynical.

"I remember C.B. as having an eclectic group of friends. He seemed to accept people for what they were," says Stefan Clausen, former Wilkes classmate, friend to C.B. and the man who literally gave him life by giving him breath in that alley. "He seemed to be a savvy kid, but still figuring out who he was."

"When I think of C.B. I'm always reminded to appreciate what you have," says Jamie Wecker, teacher and football coach at Towanda. The two grew up together, played football together and were even at Wilkes together, a few feet apart on that balcony when everything changed for C.B. "I tell my students it only takes a second to change your life and, just like that, you've got a whole new set of challenges."

It could have been Wecker who took that fall. He was standing in front of that same railing minutes before C.B. took over the spot, engaging in a conversation with Clausen. Wecker was one reason C.B. was not only a student at Wilkes but playing football for the Colonels. The other was his high school football coach, Jack Young, who put in a good word for him with Wilkes Coach Joe DeMelfi who had talked to C.B. about playing football there when he was in high school.

C.B. had always been the most laid back, the most athletic and the least scholarly of the Miller siblings. As much as he excelled at sports, he was something of an underachiever as a student. C.B. had an innate intelligence, which frustrated teachers who were concerned that he may have been wasting his potential. It may have had something to do with his sibling closest in age, Kathie, the family brain. The comparisons started in the primary grades of his Catholic elementary school, St. Agnes, with Kathie only a couple of grades ahead of him, and anything he did academically or creatively was never as good as what she had done or was doing. Sports, on the other hand, set him apart from the beginning. He may have looked like the chubby kid who couldn't keep up, but looks, as they say, can be deceiving. The desire to compete that went untapped in the classroom was fueled when he was playing basketball, baseball and later swimming and football.

He remembers an important high school football game against a league rival, Canton, and they were getting pummeled late in the game after holding a halftime lead. C.B. was on the sidelines steaming with frustration and anger, and someone in the stands—one of their own fans— was letting them have it. C.B. turned and yelled, venting his frustration, letting it all out on that fan.

"I shouldn't have done that," he says, shaking his head at the memory. "I don't get worked up much because I'm very, very calm." He pauses, rubbing his bloodshot left eye with the forefinger of his left hand. "Sometimes I got loud." He made it a point to apologize after the game. They lost, 22-9, but he seems to regret his interaction with the fan more than the outcome of the game.

"He was just an unbelievable athlete," says a high school rival and college teammate, Damon "Boo" Perry, who was a four-year starter at quarterback for Wilkes. "He jokes about being slow, but he actually had deceptive speed and quick feet, especially for a guy his size."

Athletic ability wasn't C.B.'s only gift. He also had a natural talent for making people laugh, a skill that led him to have a reputation for being a class clown. For every teacher who found his sense of humor refreshing, there was another who regarded it as an impediment to what he or she was trying to accomplish in the classroom. It's interesting to note, however, that none regarded him as a troublemaker because there was not a malicious bone in his rather substantial body.

Little did he know that years later, when the rest of his high school classmates had embarked on careers that left high school far behind them, C.B. would be sitting in these same classrooms as an adult, relearning forgotten lessons that once came easily to him. Now, because all but the most basic reading and writing skills had been destroyed, he had to absorb everything orally. That was the learning channel that was open, full-throttle open as it turns out.

While athletics and clowning around might have been C.B.'s primary pursuits throughout high school—sometimes at the cost of better grades—he did not lack a promising future when he graduated. He planned to attend college and become a teacher. He started to pursue this plan, but even the best laid plans can take detours. And C.B.'s life plan took one, even before that fateful night in July 1994.

Taking a detour with baseball, alcohol

C.B. started his college life at the Penn State branch campus in Hazleton, PA, where he played baseball for the school's team. Baseball was his favorite sport. He loved to defend the perimeters of first base with his quick feet and deft glove. His quickness didn't translate into speed on the base paths—C.B. likes to say they had to use a calendar to time his base running. He could pound the ball at the plate, as his old high school baseball coach, Bill Sexton, will tell you. He could hit for average as well as power. Sexton says that one of C.B.'s towering home runs still ranks as one of the most impressive he's witnessed from the dugout.

"I hit some of the longest singles you've ever seen," says C.B., making another playful jab at his lack of speed.

Indeed, he was living the dream at Penn State-Hazleton, playing baseball and rooming with another jock, a 21-year-old upperclassman who was showing the young freshman the ropes. Most of those ropes were hitched to partying and having a good time. C.B. got into some serious drinking and even experimented with drugs, including one, and only one, psychedelic pharmaceutical that had him fleeing from a giant ant. Alcohol was his drug of choice. It made him happy, not aggressive, and he was having such a good time that he failed to go to class, resulting in a .5 grade-point average at the end of his first semester. To put that in perspective, if he had received straight D's in his courses, he could have doubled that average.

"I went back (for the second semester) and started to do the same thing," he says ruefully of his experience on the same Penn State campus where his older brother had excelled.

He's not sure why he couldn't change his course. Had it been a baseball game and he had struck out the first three times up, he would still go to the plate believing he'd drive the next decent pitch out of the park. No such attitude emerged when it came to his studies. Make that lack of studies. Barely a week into the second semester, he called his mother and dropped the news that he wanted out. Then came the most frightening part. His mother directed him to make the same call to his father.

"It was a little scary, but Mom and Dad already knew I was not doing well." It seemed dishonest somehow, unfair to his parents, to keep up the pretense at their expense. He had been smart enough to collect decent grades in high school without much studying. "When I was at St. Agnes I studied all the time because we had nuns." He brightens at the memory of parochial elementary school, as if struck by a revelation. "That's key. What I needed were some nuns."

So he called home to tell his parents he was dropping out. That was bad enough, but their face-to-face encounter, when they came to pick him up from the modern campus on a hilltop in Luzerne County's Sugarloaf Township, was worse. C.B. was about to experience the longest, quietest ride he ever endured.

"I got in the car and my Dad said, 'Get a job or go into the Army, Navy, Air Force or Marines.' That's it. That's the only thing he said." The remainder of the two-hour drive was in silence. C.B. likes to tell that story, though it may have been the low point of his life up to that point. It's not because he is proud of it or because he is trivializing it. In a way, it shows he is pretty good when it comes to second chances. He would get another chance at college and, after that, another chance at life.

His father, as a chemist and long-time employee at the GTE-Sylvania plant in Towanda, was able to find a job for his youngest son there. Mike Miller believed in teaching lessons by actions, not preaching. You couldn't have asked for worse jobs in the plant, unless you wanted to drive home the point that perhaps a college education isn't so bad after all. For C.B., being out in the workforce was a sobering lesson, sweating out shifts doing some of the toughest jobs in the plant, notably working the cobalt furnaces.

"When I worked at GTE it woke me up real, real quick," C.B. says of his months there.

"It actually pleased us that he took himself out of school in that second semester," his father would confess years later. "It would have probably taken me another month to pick up on it."

"I'm sure it was the hardest call he ever had to make, but I am just so grateful that he realized where he was headed," says his mother. "He would have gotten into big trouble, I think."

His second chance at college came at Wilkes University. Football turned out to be the ticket in, not baseball. When you're pushing 300 pounds and you're a good athlete, a football coach at a small college with a strong football program is going to take you seriously as an offensive lineman. He wanted to be a history teacher, and he felt more at home at Wilkes whose campus lies just off center city Wilkes-Barre, blending in with neighborhoods there. Where the Penn State branch campus had been set away from the small city of Hazleton, with a nearby shopping mall and commercial strip the closest thing to a neighborhood, Wilkes was part of the community. C.B. felt at home there. He also felt he was part of a close-knit community of students. Perhaps more important was the fact that the first real failure in his young life had helped him grow up a bit.

He did at Wilkes what he hadn't in Hazleton. He attended classes and did the requisite studies and assignments. This time the grades were good, though not great. He studied as much as he had to and excelled in history and science courses. English and math were his least favorite, but he did what he had to do. Entering his junior year, just weeks before the start of fall classes, in fact, he was feeling he was on the right course, not the fish out of water he had been before.

He knew what it was like to fail but not let those failures prevent you from changing so you can succeed. Even at Wilkes, he admits he coasted at times. Penn State had taught him lessons, but he was still that kid figuring out who he was. This is probably why he feels so comfortable talking to both high school and college students today, why he feels he can motivate them.

Now a high school teacher, Wecker invites C.B. to speak to his students now and then. On one such occasion, the two naturally fell into verbal jousting, picking on each other as old friends often do. The kids, seemed to enjoy the banter between their teacher and their visitor as he shared his story. After one exchange, C.B. shook his head in mock dismay, and then, as if confiding in the students, said, "We joke because we can't cry," wiping away a mock tear from his left eye—the one that produces no tears— for dramatic effect.

These moments of humor tend to resonate with the audiences who've heard one of C.B.'s motivational talks, and they help illuminate his impressive story of recovery.

C.B. lives independently in his own apartment in his hometown Towanda and drives his own car, which has been modified to accommodate a right arm that doesn't work and a right leg that doesn't work as well as it should. He is still a big guy. He might even be intimidating if he weren't so friendly, entertaining and funny. He shares his story with others as a motivational speaker, including at-risk youngsters and classes of students at his old high school. Once a year, he holds court over a class of physical therapy students at the University of Scranton. He wants people to know that if he can come back from what he did, their perceived barriers are minor by comparison.

Obviously, he deserves much of the credit for his comeback, as do his parents and loyal friends. Throw in some luck, like a recently discharged Army combat soldier who knew what to do in the critical minutes after the fall, and having a doctor for a brother who put him in the hands of the right neurosurgeon. Being in great shape for football, less than two weeks away from grueling twice-a-day summer practices, certainly prepped him for the physical demands he would face in the summer and fall of 1994.

"My physical condition saved my life," he acknowledges.

No time to mourn what is lost

C.B. is also thankful to the many people who were there for him along the way. In many ways, he was cared for by an entire community, including some of those Wilkes students, as he went through the long process of physical therapy and other aspects of recovery.

"A lot of people give up very quickly, and that's not my game. I push myself probably better now than before I got hurt," he says when the conversation turns to what he feels he is meant to do with his life after his amazing comeback. "I'm not ready to give up. I want more."

That "more" includes pushing himself to improve physically and mentally. He is constantly on the move. Exercise and working out do not appeal to him, perhaps because of the toll of all those months of physical therapy, some of it painful and numbingly repetitive. It's not so much about him any more. What he wants is to make a difference in other lives as a living lesson. He feels he survived because he is destined to contribute something. He has something to give to others, he believes, and he has already changed some lives for the better, turned some kids around.

C.B. embraces the chance this accident has provided him to make a difference. And he's aware that the time he has to have an impact might be short. "You get so many chips in life," explains C.B.'s brother, Mike. "My brother spent a load of chips the night of his accident— a whole lot of chips. I might be the first born, but I'm no longer the oldest child in the family. My brother's got me by 15 years because of the wear and the tear and reserve that was spent."

There is no question that a brain injury shortens one's life. Susan H. Connors, President/CEO of the Brain Injury Association of America, reports that, on the average, brain injury reduces life expectancy by seven years. And that includes the gamut that fits under the definition of "an alteration in brain function, or other evidence of brain pathology, caused by an external force."

Acquired brain injury is any brain injury that occurs after birth. It includes both traumatic brain injury and non-traumatic brain injury (such as strokes, anoxia, infection, lack of oxygen and other internal factors). Of these the annual toll of TBI (1.7 million) more than doubles that of strokes (about 800,000).

"This is a disease process, not an event," Connors reported in September 2012 at the 11th Annual Northeastern U.S. Conference on Disability. In other words, it makes you more vulnerable to other diseases and accelerates those diseases when they strike. As they say in the field, it is disease causative and disease accelerative.

Even though the sense of humor is still there and C.B. is blessed with clear memories of a past that give him his identity, his brother believes that the C.B. who is with them now is another person. The trick was finding what was left of the old C.B., the quirks and the interests, and then determine what kind of support would be needed. That's the strategy of care his father assumed early on, and Michael calls it "the gold standard."

More importantly, C.B. understands that. He knows he has been reborn, and though he may treasure memories of his former life, the bonds and friendships that continue to be so important, he never seems to feel sorry for himself or wish that he could be what he had once been.

"He's been there. He stood at death's door," says the oldest of the Miller siblings. "He stood there and danced a couple times back and forth, probably because that's kind of him, that's who he is."

If this is a new person, then he was, in a sense, dancing on his own grave, celebrating the new life that was to come, not mourning lost dreams and ambitions.

In the waning days of June in 2012, C.B. learns that the neurosurgeon who presided over his treatment in the critical weeks after his accident, Dr. David J. Sedor, has died. Here was the man who, in his eyes, gave his second life new birth. Yet he never really knew him, because that time of his life has been blotted from memory. Sedor was only fifty when he died and C.B., had been one of his first major cases after completing his neurosurgical residency in 1993 at Hahnemann University Hospital in Philadelphia. This is where Sedor and another young resident at that time, Michael Miller, had something in common, namely friends and associates within the medical center. This common ground would provide someone to turn to for information and expertise, ultimately bringing Dr. Sedor into C.B.'s team. Michael cites this as a seminal moment in C.B.'s care, not only saving his brother's life but giving him a chance at something resembling a normal life.

"He thrived on taking care of each and every patient as if he were taking care of a member of his own family," Sedor's obituary stated. The Millers would enthusiastically concur with that assessment. As for C.B., he knew that someone important to his life was now gone, but without a memory connection he found it difficult to grieve.

In a poem dedicated to what was regarded as the miracle of C.B.'s recovery, and offered in the beginning of this book, Alfred S. Groh put it this way.

You do what you have to do

And stay until the job is done:

Nothing can be finished

Unless, first, it is begun.

It was Sedor, near the start of what would be a too brief career, who would give C.B. his new beginning. Groh, former Wilkes professor and husband of Dean Jane Lampe Groh, probably didn't know when he penned that verse how far C.B. would go. Nevertheless, he was prescient.

The closing line his poem, entitled "A Matter of Recovery," proclaims: "And you do what you do without fear of what's ahead!"

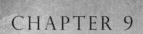

CHAPTER 9

A SLOW START AND TIME RUNNING OUT

The going was slow for C.B. Miller in October and November of 1994, with the shadow of a deadline looming over a crucial phase of his recovery. The early stages of rehabilitation were critical in gauging whether he could expect to live an independent and meaningful life in the wake of traumatic brain injury. The odds, again, were not in his favor. He had already beaten some heavy ones merely by surviving his crushing injuries. Now, how much he would benefit from physical and occupational therapy remained a towering question mark.

In retrospect, it is easy to understand why C.B.'s caseworker, Donna Kopicki, had not been particularly hopeful that the stocky young man in her charge would advance beyond much more than minimal awareness and capabilities. Yet there was something about him. Professional detachment is especially important for caseworkers and therapists working with the brain injured. It's not that they can't get up close and personal, or even show affection, but they typically keep professional distance, striving not to take patients and their tragic circumstances home with them, so to speak.

When C.B. arrived at rehab, Kopicki assessed him for what she could see in her new patient. She noted that he could barely communicate, limited to yes/no responses that weren't very reliable—sometimes he'd say yes when he meant no and vice versa. And often, he'd express himself using gestures and facial expressions rather than words. At first glance, based on what could be seen as he arrived in her care, C.B. seemed destined for either skilled nursing or home health care. Kopicki might have imagined his future as living with his parents until they were unable to provide the assistance he needed, an unfortunate scenario seen too often in young people struck down by TBI. His injuries were amongst the most extreme she'd seen in patients being rehabbed at Heinz.

Those first few weeks at Heinz offered no indication of a miraculous recovery. C.B. was there a month and a half before achieving one of his greatest accomplishments— uttering of three words that were strung together to create his first complete sentence.

The specific question that provoked the response has been forgotten, but what he said was this: "I don't know." That was it— a confession of ignorance perhaps, but enlightening nonetheless. All parties involved were overjoyed, but the celebration was short-lived. Time was running out for C.B. at Heinz. At a time when it seemed they were just beginning to make real progress, shaking loose the words that had been trapped inside his brain. Mike Miller could see the door to recovery and independence starting to open, and he wasn't about to allow it to slam shut.

In his early fifties at the time, Mike was known as a facilitator, a leader who gets the most out of people united in a cause. That's a valuable asset when your son is in the early stages of recovery from traumatic brain injury. Armed with exemplary organizational skills, once he sets a goal he will not stop until he achieves it. But he is also human, and the stress of the situation was starting to catch up to him. He was exhausted, on edge, sleep deprived, not eating properly and experiencing digestive problems.

And there, always nagging at him, were the uncertainties regarding C.B.'s future, including financial, legal and, most importantly, quality of life.

"This turned into a very stressful time," Mike explains. "As we watched him struggle for words, attempt even the most basic tasks, or find out that he had lost the hearing in his left ear, my feelings were on the surface. I don't mean that I would break down, but I could feel the emotions well up in me at the slightest provocation."

He tried to balance these conflicting feelings by forcing himself to stay positive. He and Sharon exulted in anything that seemed to advance C.B.'s recovery, no matter how simple or seemingly insignificant.

"We struggled… and we struggled often," Mike recalls of those first two months at Heinz. "We felt very low. And this was compounded by a schedule that involved work, driving back and forth to Wilkes-Barre, trying to keep up with all of the issues surrounding his accident. You know, the legal stuff, guardianship, power of attorney and trying to figure out what we're going to do when he's discharged from rehab. It all left me feeling totally exhausted most of the time."

The team of doctors, caseworkers and therapists at the rehab center would hold regular staff meetings for each of their patients. Family members were invited to these sessions as a courtesy. Mike and Sharon Miller chose to attend, because the better they knew the staff, each team member's nuances and how they might react to certain situations, the more informed their decisions could be. Mike Miller was the consummate team player, but, also being a man accustomed to taking a leadership role, he was not afraid to challenge a call or strategy that seemed ill advised. If it meant being outspoken, he'd do it, ruffling as few feathers as possible but remaining mindful of the urgency of his son's plight, as well as dedicated to doing all he could to steer it in a positive direction.

"I don't know if any other patients' families went to their team meetings," Mike Miller says, looking back, "but it proved to be critical for the challenges we'd have to face."

The Millers discovered that the meetings were refreshingly inclusive. Their comments, observations and suggestions were welcomed by the staff. The Millers were there for candid appraisals of their son's progress and, in some cases, the lack of it.

Occupational therapy addresses the patient's ability to complete everyday activities such as getting in and out of bed, putting on shoes and clothing or any of a number of activities most people do every day without much effort or thought. Among rehabilitation professionals, these are referred to as "activities of daily living," and they are key to someone being able to live an independent life. For C.B., with his right arm and hand of little use and the source of considerable pain and his right leg providing limited movement, these sessions were demanding, exhausting and often exasperating.

Occupational therapy is a process of evaluations and establishing goals, And, as the Millers were to discover, it sets the table for the direction and scope of the recovery of a brain-injured patient.

"All of the therapies (physical, occupational, cognitive and speech) were very difficult for him, but both physical and occupational therapies were also incredibly painful," his father recalls. C.B.'s expressions and body language, his chief tools of communication at the time, made this clear. But Mike sensed something else was going on with C.B. Even though he had put up an admirable fight to get where he was, C.B. was suddenly unwilling to attend sessions with his occupational therapist. The occupational therapist herself was espousing the opinion that fear of pain was behind his lack of cooperation.

During one of the staff meetings when the team was discussing C.B.'s case, the occupational therapist clinically noted that the sessions tended to be difficult and very challenging, as well as painful. She went on to suggest that C.B. wasn't doing well in the sessions because of the pain he was experiencing. C.B. was also present at the meetings, and members of the team tried to convince him that he would have to deal with the pain and work through it to complete the sessions if he expected to reap any gains. Even though C.B. could not respond to these team directives, his parents could see the frustration of a young man who wanted to shout out, "No, that isn't the problem!"

Unfortunately, Mike and Sharon could not confirm or refute this because C.B. remained unable to articulate his feelings. The expressive aphasia was making it difficult for C.B. to express anything, let alone the complicated feelings of frustration and disagreement with what an entire team of professionals was presenting. One thing Mike did know: as an athlete, his son had never backed away from challenges. Yet he still had misgivings about how much of the old C.B. remained inside that traumatized brain.

An old fear returned, one that had stalked him during the desperate days when C.B. was fighting for his life at the hospital. Would the person who eventually emerged from this journey of rediscovery be a stranger inside the body of his son? Would they be mourning the death of someone they had loved for twenty-one years and, at the same time, welcoming a stranger into their lives? Despite the signs that the old C.B. was still in there, a personality trapped like a genie in a lamp, his father had not forgotten a decision he had reached weeks before at the hospital.

"We needed to mourn the fact that we may have lost C.B. as we knew him and be prepared to find out who the new person is that comes out of this coma," he had vowed. "The possibilities were endless, but there was also the chance his personality would be completely different when he awoke."

Mike was prepared for the possibility that C.B. would never fully recover from his brain injury, that they must appreciate and accept whatever is retrieved and proceed from there. This realization had come after some long periods of reflection and prayer. As aggressive and tireless as he had vowed to be in helping his son become independent, the spiritual part of him had come to terms with another source of empowerment —acceptance. If, in the end, it was not meant to be, they would accept it and move on. Que sera, sera.

Mike took to describing the challenges they faced as rediscovery. The process involved elements of rehabilitation, recovery, even healing, but it was not limited to those elements. Along the way, C.B. must not only recover but rediscover what he would become in his second chance at life. At the same time, those who loved him would also come to know the C.B. who emerged from the darkness and rebuilt his personal library. Everyone would come to accept this process and what it required.

Acceptance was one thing, but Mike Miller, the pragmatist, also understood that some obstacles had to be conquered. Such was the case with what appeared to be a roadblock in C.B.'s comeback. These occupational therapy sessions were not only critical, there was little time to waste.

C.B. didn't need to speak in clear sentences for his father to come to the conclusion that his stubborn reluctance to cooperate with this therapist was not about pain.

"Of course it was painful for him to do the exercises in occupational therapy, but I was becoming more convinced that it had more to do with personality problems with the therapist. I do not know to this day what caused it but he did not seem to connect with the therapist, or perhaps her style."

This presented Mike with a touchy issue to address. C.B.'s obvious discomfort and frustration with the treatment team's increasing acceptance of the occupational therapist's conclusion told his father the subject needed to be broached. At the same time, Mike was aware that he must not come across as the narrow-minded parent looking for a scapegoat, someone to blame for his son not progressing as he should. Casting an ominous shadow over all of this was an urgency to resolve this dilemma, "because we were on a schedule determined in a large way by how much our insurance would fund." In other words, he could not allow the rehab process to stall as they debated the cause for this one setback.

Sometimes It's All about Chemistry...

Mike proceeded cautiously and, he hoped, kindly, with his theory on what might be the cause for this impediment in C.B.'s progress. It was based on a simple truth: Sometimes two people lack chemistry. No one is at fault for the failure in the relationship. It is merely human nature. We're drawn to some people and not so much to others. This chemistry forms the unique bonds of friendship. It can also be how teachers connect with certain students.

Hoping he had eliminated the elements of blame and failure from the critique by establishing this premise, Mike put his proposition on the table:

"I proposed that the fastest way to test my theory was to change therapists for the next session. If it was a personality issue between this therapist and C.B, he would participate in the therapy immediately. If he balked with the new therapist, then we could conclude that the issue was the pain associated with the therapy. Either way, we'd have the information we needed to move forward, one way or the other."

The team, after some discussion, agreed to do as Mike suggested.

"After we left the meeting, we took C.B. back to his room," Mike remembers. "When we got there he thanked me for speaking up. He still could not speak effectively, but it was obvious from the expression on his face what he was trying to say. The next day he attended all of his therapy sessions and never missed another one."

C.B. remembers this as one of his most difficult challenges in rehab. "My right hand was very, very painful, and people were thinking

I was not working because it hurt," he recalls. The real problem was something he couldn't convey because he basically had a two-word vocabulary at the time— yes and no. Because he wasn't talking, the therapist wasn't saying anything to him during their sessions together. There was nothing to motivate him, which made the pain and his frustration with it even more oppressive. When C.B. refused to attend one of the sessions, it brought the situation to a head. He was grateful his father was able to pick up on the nuances of the situation. With a change in therapists to one who opened a much needed channel of communication, C.B. was able to concentrate on the goals of the therapy instead of fixating on the immediate, demanding challenges of each session.

"It's not that it was all fun and games with another therapist, or anything like that," he says today. "I still didn't want to do it, but I did it anyway because it had to be done."

The important outcome of this intervention was that C.B.'s comeback was back on track. He suddenly seemed to be clicking, gaining ground on all fronts with his various therapies. Some of those entrapped words, bottled by aphasia, were starting to free themselves and bubble to the surface.

That victory brought enormous relief, but there was an even more pressing battle awaiting Mike Miller as winter approached in 1994 with little time to resolve it. He learned that their insurer would no longer pay for the inpatient therapy at Heinz, that services would be terminated in a matter of days. It had been little more than four months since C.B.'s accident, and it seemed that the most significant gains were just starting to unfold.

In early December, a social worker at Heinz delivered the bad news: They had no choice but to discharge C.B. the following week. Even though the treatment staff at Heinz concurred that he could still benefit from inpatient services, there was no way that could be provided without the insurer picking up the tab. It seemed someone at the insurance company had made the decision that inpatient rehab was no longer warranted. In truth, this was more likely an automatic termination, sticking to a formula that had seldom been contested.

Up to that point, Kopicki had never had a patient who was covered beyond the standard two months before being discharged to outpatient status. Members of the team dealing with C.B. were treatment specialists with little or no contact with the insurers paying the bills for their services. Social workers at Heinz were the closest to being intermediaries, but their chief concern was dealing with the patients and their families, helping them make the transition to either outpatient treatment or assisting them in facilitating the next level of care. Their challenge was to accomplish as much as they could over the course of the limited time given them.

That left it up to Mike Miller to deal with the insurance company. He entered the fray armed with some valuable knowledge he had gleaned about dealing with insurers.

One thing was clear from the start: Mike Miller was not about to accept rejection, especially knowing that the staff at Heinz would back him up. He had learned that he had the right to appeal any decision affecting health-care services provided to or denied his son. He was told there were several levels of appeal, starting with a basic appeal of his own. If that was rejected, he could have an attending physician make a request in writing on his behalf, which would be reviewed by the HMO's medical director.

When told that the process became "more complicated" from that point on, he asked the inevitable question: "I assume that by complicated you mean that it could involve lawyers?"

That assumption was confirmed and Mike Miller would appeal, appeal and appeal again. Social services at Heinz made the initial appeal at his request. A Heinz social worker agreed to do so after cautioning him that insurers never reverse decisions on terminating services. Sure enough, they were subsequently informed that the appeal was denied.

"I then asked her to have the physiatrist at John Heinz contact the HMO and make the appeal," he said. "Again she cautioned me that this is not their usual procedure and reminded me that the HMO never reverses this kind of decision." But they did as he requested, with the result being another rejection.

Mike was like a batter with two strikes against him, knowing the next pitch will result in either a strikeout or a home run to win the game. Now was the time to step up to the plate.

The next call Mike made was to his lawyer in Philadelphia. After filling him in on the situation with the HMO provider, Mike heard in reply "let me see what I can do." What he could do became apparent before the end of the next day, virtually on the eve of C.B. being cut loose.

"I got a call from Heinz telling me that C.B.'s stay would be extended for another two months." That was huge, and an overjoyed Mike Miller relayed his heartfelt appreciation to the attorney. He never did find out what his attorney did to get them to agree to an extension, but he did learn a valuable lesson: "Use all levels of appeal when dealing with service providers and insurance companies." You don't walk back to the dugout with just one or two strikes.

Setting the Stage for Independence...

The year of C.B.'s accident was the 28th anniversary year of Mike and Sharon Miller's marriage. During those years Mike had worked his way up at the GTE Sylvania plant in Towanda, working under several different corporate owners. It took him twelve years, taking college courses in the evenings while holding down a full time job to earn a bachelor's degree in chemistry, advancing him to engineer's status. His work ethic and skills impressed his employers so much that they offered him a fellowship under which he was able to earn a master's degree. This launched his career into a management role, as well as significantly boosting his level of pay.

His career and income gains may have been belated, but by 1994 he was making a comfortable salary, having already assisted three of his four children through college. As for Sharon, she had been a stay-at-home mom, taking care of other people's kids on the side, until Michael, the oldest, went off to college. She then returned to a former role as administrative assistant for the regional office of a telephone company.

They seemed poised for a secure financial future, eyeing retirement just a few years down the road, but C.B.'s accident changed everything. By the time C.B. was at John Heinz, Mike was back on the job, making the long drive between Towanda and Wilkes-Barre when he wasn't working. In addition, he was doing all he could to ensure that his brain-injured son would himself be financially secure in the coming years.

"We went from a situation where we had all of our kids either finished with college or most of the way through it, and we were actually getting used to and enjoying some of the aspects of 'empty-nest syndrome,'" he said of that hectic summer and fall. "Now we had to consider the lifelong care of our 21-year-old son. It really was exhausting and scary."

Part of their plans for securing C.B.'s long-term future involved hiring the best legal representation they could find. That process included the prerequisite research and interviewing the firms at the top of their list. Among the recommendations was a firm in Philadelphia that offered a wide range of services often required in situations like C.B.'s and had represented many clients with liability issues. An intimate knowledge of the nuances of Pennsylvania law was also critical, and, again, the firm fit the bill.

C.B.'s future was still questionable back then. His parents would pursue any legal matters, such as pursuing cases of liability and establishing a trust for C.B., with the goal of guaranteeing him "at least a reasonable lifestyle." They based their definition of "reasonable" on the projected income of a high school teacher since that had been C.B.'s career goal as a college junior.

The law firm took on the Millers' case and reported their findings. They concluded that there were four avenues of liability they could potentially pursue: the owner of the building, the city of Wilkes-Barre, the university and the college students renting the apartment where the accident occurred.

Mike and Sharon quickly dismissed the idea of pursuing cases against either Wilkes University or the students. They turned their legal counsel's attention toward the owner of the building and the city of Wilkes-Barre, which had a number of citations on record against the owner and might not have aggressively pursued corrective action.

"We decided against a shotgun approach to liability, striking at all possible targets," Mike said. "Our goals were modest, not vindictive. we refused to make room for any vindictive feelings."

What he concluded, after a studied examination of the accident and circumstances surrounding it, was that the property owner was clearly negligent: "He had operated a rental property he knew was dangerous. The porch on the other side of the building had collapsed shortly before C.B.'s accident."

In just a matter of weeks, Mike Miller had successfully conducted campaigns that resulted in extending inpatient treatment at the rehabilitation hospital of their choice, followed by what would be many more months of out-patient therapy there. In addition, the Millers hired a law firm that would help them establish a trust that would provide life-long support for their brain-injured son.

Their resolute pursuit of any and all information that would spare them heartache and expense along the way included learning from another father of a young man with TBI that Mike should pursue becoming the legal guardian of C.B. Without having such authority, he could lose out on hundreds of thousands of dollars in prospective benefits for C.B. It is a step Mike urges parents of young adults with traumatic brain injury to consider.

So much was accomplished during that handful of months following C.B.'s fall, and there would be so much more on their long journey of rediscovery.

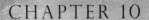

CHAPTER 10

FINDING THE WORDS FOR RECOVERY

Over the twenty years since his accident, C.B. Miller has been a regular visitor to his old haunts at the John Heinz Institute of Rehabilitation Medicine, making the trip to Wilkes-Barre almost on a monthly basis. This place came to feel like his second home, and the therapists and caseworkers there are like family. While there, C.B. essentially awakened to his second life, facing painful trials and glorious triumphs alike. In more than a symbolic way, he came of age there, over the course of four months as a patient and another full year undergoing outpatient therapy.

One of the therapists who played a key role in C.B.'s recovery at Heinz is Alexanne Kennedy Conklin. "She turned my life around. She was my savior," C.B. says earnestly of Conklin, who was his speech therapist. "She's the one who helped me get the words out."

Actually, the words didn't come during those first four months at Heinz. What Conklin did, the Millers believe, was begin the process of freeing up the logjam of words inside C.B.'s injured brain. "Early stimulation is the key," Conklin agrees.

At the time, C.B. was mostly silent, but his facial expressions and gestures revealed that there were words behind them, just waiting to be freed. As it turned out, getting the words out was going to take a lot more time.

"The speech came later, after he left me," says Conklin, who, at the age of thirty-one, had been at Heinz for about seven years when she first met C.B. "I was worried that he would never have any functional language at all."

Conklin remembers that C.B's expressive aphasia was more pronounced than that of most other TBI patients at Heinz. There was massive damage to the left frontal area of C.B.'s brain, the area that is the repository of speech. The effects of aphasia are usually more temporary in acute trauma patients, so when C.B. showed slow progress, there was reason for Conklin to be worried. C.B. would eventually make an amazing recovery... It was just going to take a long time to get there.

"He was like a big Teddy bear," Conklin says of the patient she worked with for all of those months. "Even without speaking, he was very expressive in a lot of ways."

The results of speech therapy would reveal themselves slowly, over the course of several months, even years. Most of the visible gains from inpatient therapy at Heinz emanated from the hard work of physical and occupational therapy. But even those gains were initially hindered by C.B.'s lack of verbal skills. Being unable to communicate effectively with therapists made it difficult for him, but it also made it difficult for the therapists. C.B. experienced the greatest gains thanks to the skills of therapists like Kim Jacques, who talked and reacted verbally to him even when his aphasia kept him from fully engaging in dialogue.

As C.B. neared the end of his extended stay at Heinz, the physical changes were notable. He had transitioned from a bed-ridden patient barely able to stand on his own to someone capable of walking. The impact of speech and cognitive therapies were much more difficult to evaluate. Clearly some doors were opening; his limited responses and expressions revealed thought processes and evidence of cognitive capabilities. If you ask C.B. today what his greatest frustration was then, it's as if the response takes him back in time, along with the struggle for words:

"Speech... Speech was [long pause] my enemy. I didn't know what I was doing. Alexanne took her time because I was very, very frustrated. I've got it in my brain. But when I speak sometimes I get mixed-up words and [long pause, followed by a frustrated sigh]... Alexanne helped me out tremendously, without pushing."

It may have seemed to him that she wasn't pushing, but as a speech therapist, it was Conklin's job to push the proverbial envelope. Her challenge was to get C.B. to open that envelope and reveal the message trapped inside. By the time C.B. transitioned to outpatient therapy, Conklin wasn't so sure she'd met the challenge.

"There is a lot of emotion with acute trauma patients," Conklin said. "What has happened was very sudden, unexpected, and the whole family is involved."

C.B.'s family was more involved than most, she recalls, and she describes his father as "a wonderful advocate for him." She may have forgotten some details over twenty years, but she has many clear memories of C.B.

"He came across as a stroke patient in many ways," she says of his symptoms, notably his expressive aphasia. "People with brain injury usually don't have pervasive aphasia. He was far from a typical case."

That's pervasive as in persistent and all-encompassing. He showed signs of excellent cognition skills. He would joke with his facial expressions, using his good arm to pretend he was pushing or hitting her to make a point. He liked to tease. He came to her with a feeding tube and one of the first things they had to work on was his dysphagia, or difficulty in swallowing. She remembers having to bribe him to get him to swallow his first bites of food.

"Many patients with brain injury have a swallowing dysfunction," Conklin explains. "Before we could tackle speech issues, we had to get him to swallow effectively."

Even though she is no longer working at Heinz, Conklin has seen C.B. over the years and is overjoyed by his amazing transformation. It is truly miraculous, and she is pleased that her hard work—and stimulation— may have played a part in it all.

She says a big thing C.B. has going for him is self-awareness. She believes that's why he continues to improve in his speech and language skills even to this day. He can, and will, tell you when he doesn't understand something. That's crucial in any learning process.

"It's not just me. A lot of people have the same problem," C.B. says of the aphasia that continues to be a challenge. Yet, at the time, he must have felt dreadfully alone. "I got through it with, ah, persistence— wow that's a big word— and I was very lucky."

Even though C.B. wasn't talking when his speech therapy started, Conklin seemed to understand him, to know what words were in there, waiting to be released from the grips of aphasia. Once the release of words began, a tremendous burden was lifted, freeing C.B. to be more spontaneous. That's when his rehab leaped forward.

Many of C.B.'s former caseworkers and therapists are still at Heinz, including Kopicki, who has come to consider C.B. part of her real family. She has watched C.B.'s comeback over the years, and she appreciates how far he has come. Every journey, as the proverb tells us, begins with a step, and this traveler proved small steps can result in long strides.

"When I started going to outpatient, it was a long, grueling day, but I got through it," C.B. says today. During this part of his recovery, C.B. endured more than just hours of therapy five days a week. The trip to Heinz required three hours on the road. That made for some very long days, especially for a TBI survivor whose stamina is compromised. And C.B. couldn't have done it without the help of the volunteer drivers from his home town. He still is amazed that all those people, were there for him and his parents.

A Sign of Recovery— and It's No Joke…

Sharon and Mike Miller could see something else returning in their son, and he didn't need to express himself with words to show it.

Humor had always been a constant in the Miller household. Some might even say it's a trait passed from one generation to the next, and even as a young child, C.B. seemed to have a gift for it.

"When we realized that C.B.'s sense of humor was still there, we were ecstatic and thanked God for allowing us this miracle," Mike says. Early fears about a radical personality change as a result of the brain injury were assuaged when they saw signs of that familiar sense of humor. Even simple gestures and facial expressions rang true of C.B.'s signature style of humor and impeccable comedic timing. As the words started coming out, sporadically and in short bursts, it only strengthened the belief that the C.B. was still there, finding his way back to the surface.

C.B. had always been able to make his mother laugh, sometimes evading her anger or discipline by doing so. It was something that sister, Kathie, says she both admired and resented when they were growing up.

"He used humor to his advantage," she said, recalling how he got away with things she and her other siblings couldn't. Like the time her mother was supposed to be chewing C.B. out: "She tried, but she couldn't keep a straight face because C.B. found a way to make her laugh while she was trying to set him straight. Of course, being a teenager at the time, I kept thinking it wasn't fair… he was able to distract her and evade punishment."

And yet nobody was happier than his sister to learn her brother's sense of humor, the source of occasional sibling envy during childhood, had not been extinguished or altered.

During C. B.'s first week at Heinz, he discovered the button that raised and lowered his bed. He had been told to call a nurse if he needed a change in position, but he took matters into his one healthy hand, laughing gleefully as the bed went up and down. By the end of November there was no question that at least some of his sense of humor had survived.

In another example of those early signs of humor, when somebody said something about patience in a conversation, C.B. responded without missing a beat and with a little playful twinkle in his eye, "It's a virtue." Such a reaction draws on memory and connects concepts together to deliver a line with the timing of a stand-up comic, whether intentional or instinctive. You're either funny or you are not, as any class clown will tell you, and apparently this class clown still had it.

More importantly, the emergence of humor seemed to be the vehicle that would drive C.B.'s comeback as a communicator. Complete thoughts expressed in short sentences demonstrated that he was not only grasping what was going on around him but was taking it an extra step in that mysterious process known as humor. It hadn't been destroyed with those millions of so-called brain cells (actually neurons or nerve cells) claimed in his fall.

Signs that C.B. was starting to conquer the aphasia, recapture vocabulary and regain analytical skills inherent in humor were promising, even exhilarating, at times. The process continues, proving that conventional thinking may have been wrong back in the day when they put caps on the recovery of people with traumatic brain injury. Learning continues through a lifetime, even if it is someone, like C. B. Miller, who was blessed with the opportunity to live a second life.

Far too often, the brain injured end up "discharged to the couch," as they say in the field. This refers to patients being released from rehab and sent home or to a facility like a nursing home where there are few or no ongoing therapy or activities designed to help them continue to make progress. As the Millers learned, the fate of someone in desperate need of rehab may be in the hands of a system not set up to deal with the complexities involved in the individualized nature of brain injuries.

"Some arbitrary payer has decided there will be no further treatment," says the woman at the helm of the Brain Injury Association of America, Susan H. Connors. "What the system is telling you is, 'We saved your life. Now we're going to kick you over the cliff.'"

Had that attitude prevailed in the case of C. B. Miller, he, too, might be in a nursing or personal care facility today. Fortunately for C.B., he had someone who took on the role of his advocate, refusing to accept the status quo. Most people with TBI don't have someone like Mike Miller in their corner, someone who sees challenges, not obstacles, someone who finds a way to "yes" when everyone around him is saying "no."

"People are being discharged way too early," says Conklin, of the rehab process for the traumatically injured. There is often too little time, dictated by insurance caps, to give patients a fair start on the comeback trail. Not all TBI survivors have the persistence of C.B. Miller and the commitment of family members to treat rehabilitation as a lifelong learning process. Too often the rehabilitation—and learning—will stall, if not cease completely, once discharged from a place like Heinz.

Conklin intimated that this frustration is one reason why she is now applying her therapeutic skills to elderly patients in their finals days, their brains under attack by internal non-traumatic invaders like stroke and Alzheimer's.

They, unlike many of her acute trauma patients over twenty-three years at Heinz, got to enjoy normal and productive lives before aging took its toll.

CHAPTER 11

COMING BACK AS
A COLLEGE BOY

One year after C.B.'s accident, in late July 1995, the Miller family hosted what they called, "a celebration of life," to thank everyone who had helped them in the early stages of C.B.'s comeback. Yes, he was coming back, and there may have been a long way to go, but there were plenty of reasons to be thankful and celebrate.

More than 200 people attended the gathering in Towanda. They came from Wilkes University, Wilkes-Barre General Hospital and John Heinz Rehab, along with volunteers, family and friends from Towanda, the Millers' hometown.

"There truly are so many wonderful people willing to help when given the opportunity," Sharon Miller said of the many who've helped over the years, joining in one or many stages of C.B.'s journey.

Sylvia Radway Abrams wasn't part of that celebration, but she would soon find herself playing a major role in C.B.'s comeback.

C.B. was embarking on part of his journey that didn't have a map. Moving beyond rehabilitation, he and his parents had to decide where to go next. Physically, C.B. had reclaimed most of what he could expect to get back. He may be classified as "disabled," but the Miller mindset was that he would be facing challenges, not handicaps. Challenges could be met and conquered. A handicap, by its definition, was something you accepted as your lot in life. You worked around a handicap, which is defined as a hindrance. A handicap is also defined as a mechanism for evening up a competition—to help someone compete against a more gifted performer. Disabled people do not like to be called handicapped, and it has nothing to do with political correctness. Being disabled, mentally or physically, brings you back to the word "challenge." Being disabled, to be blunt, means you are not able to perform specific tasks the way most people perform them. Being handicapped implies that you are able, though perhaps not expected to perform those tasks the way most people do.

C.B. had already adapted to taking care of himself using his non-dominant left arm and compensating for his compromised right leg. While he might have reached some physical limits to his recovery, there would be no such parameters on how much he might recapture from a brain that was literally rewiring itself. His brain was still striving to assign old familiar functions to new places, bridging new and circumventing old pathways amidst a vast mass of lifeless cells.

The celebration of this one-year milestone, this show of love and appreciation, was really about commemorating what was just the beginning, as far as C.B. and his parents were concerned. The first leg of the journey had been both draining and energizing; it tested their collective will but found them more than up to the challenge. At times they had been demoralized and despondent, at others they found themselves inspired and triumphant. They expected nothing else from the rest of the journey.

The compass that guided the course of C.B.'s comeback was C.B. himself— not somebody else's expectations of how far he might go. Mike, always searching for ways to ensure C.B.'s continued progress and improve his odds of living productively, had settled on the "person controlled model" approach. The accident was traumatic and put C.B. on a new, unchartered course. But C.B. was still the captain of his own ship. And Mike set out to help C.B. discover what he wanted to do with his new life and hoped to provide the tools to get him there. Failure was nothing to fear, even if the goal seemed far-fetched.

When asked what he wanted most, C.B. consistently expressed a desire for an education. He wanted to complete his pursuit of a college diploma. As limited as his vocabulary was at the time he left rehab, success in the classroom might have been dismissed as a pipe dream. With his limited ability to read and write, attaining his goal of a degree would be like rebuilding an engine with only a pair of pliers.

Rather than relying on traditional ways of teaching and learning, educating C.B. would require oral learning, and that demanded a tool C.B. had in abundance—memory. At first, due to his expressive aphasia, no one recognized just how powerful that tool was in C.B.. His memory had somehow been virtually undiminished by the massive trauma to the frontal lobe, which sits above and to the front of the temporal lobe, which houses the dual functions of memory and the capacity to understand language.

Mike recruited a team of local educators, asking them to serve as advisors in helping C.B. reach his goal. That team was comprised of a number of teachers, volunteer tutors from the regional literacy program and even the Towanda school district superintendent. Most of them were familiar with C.B., either from his days as a student or from knowing the Miller family.

With input from these volunteers, a game plan took shape. It started with C.B. auditing high school classes. After about a year and a half of that, he then would audit selected college courses at a nearby satellite program used mostly for adult education. The team would monitor C.B.'s progress, meet with him regularly and make recommendations. A few years after sitting in on that first high school class, he enrolled in a weekender program provided by Keystone College at a Towanda satellite facility. From there it would take eleven years to get his bachelor's degree.

At the time of the one-year celebration, none of this was known. In fact, the Millers and their friends were simply appreciating the fact that C.B. had survived. They were still taking it one day at a time. But with a window on C.B.'s future opening more with each passing day, they could see a road stretch out before them, a road of promise and potential. Many guides would come along to offer assistance and help them realize that potential. One of them was Sylvia Abrams.

Abrams, a teacher, had known C.B. before but mostly as a likeable classmate of her daughter, Susan. When C.B. had his accident, Sylvia's own son was getting ready for his freshman year of college. She was a middle school reading specialist. Her classroom was next to that of a member of the "education committee," and she got reacquainted with C.B. during the period when he was monitoring classes.

Sylvia Abrams was working with C.B. when he committed himself to going back to college. She accomplished their shared goal of rebuilding his vocabulary by using a unique process one might describe as engineered especially for someone who would have to rely mostly on learning and testing orally.

"I never would have succeeded in finishing college if I hadn't had that step," C.B. says. And today he is the proud holder of a Bachelor of Science degree in Business Administration, minoring in human resources, from Keystone College.

Thinking back on the time she was working with C.B., Abrams recalls: "I didn't know many clinical things about him at the time, other than he had a serious brain injury from an accident a year or so before. I believe I was recommended to help C.B. get the reading instruction he'd need to fulfill his dream of taking college courses."

Even while completing his degree, C.B. never became much of a reader. What he did do is achieve a unique kind of literacy. Abrams discovered that C.B. was essentially rendered illiterate by his brain injuries; his reading and writing skills were virtually nil. Yet he had something she could work with: "a solid memory and the ability to learn orally," she said.

When Abrams started working with him more than a year after the accident, C.B. had a working vocabulary of perhaps 50 words. With the right approach, she knew she could help him expand and grow his vocabulary. She also felt he would need to recognize written words and regain at least some of his reading skills. At that point, he was a long way from being able to survive a college course, let alone pass one.

Learning Becomes a Two-Way Street...

Abrams first thought she was dealing with a case of alexia, which is the loss of the acquired ability to read due to brain injury and generally regarded as a visual form of aphasia. Her initial approach was to teach C.B. to read, rather than build his vocabulary. Once she started, however, she realized a focus on relearning how to read wasn't working. She ended up being what C.B. sees her as today—his speech teacher.

In essence, that's what she became. She focused on speech because he processes information orally. Her work with him would prove to be helpful when he returned to college studies. He wouldn't be reading when he started taking courses; lessons would be recorded or read to him by his father. Mike would spend long hours in the evenings, reading to C.B. from the textbooks, as well as transcribing the recordings of his classroom lectures. Fortunately for both of them, they eventually discovered software known as the Kurzweil Reader. Not only does it clearly read aloud the content of printed documents, but it will do the same with digital text accessed directly over the internet, including email.

Before C.B. and his parents would invest great amounts of time and effort over the course of eleven years for a college degree, C.B. and Abrams focused on improving his speech and arming him with a broader vocabulary.

"I never had any idea how injured or damaged his brain was. We just proceeded," Abrams explains. "The greatest benefit came from the fact that I was outside of his family, even though he has a great deal of love and respect for all of them," she explains, pointing out that interaction with someone other than his family was important for his development. He needed someone other than family who could validate him and provide confirmation that he was on the right path and that he could succeed.

It is said of people who teach the learning disabled that the best are the ones willing to learn from their students. In other words, Sylvia Abrams had to learn lessons about C.B. Miller and how to reach him before she could actually teach him effectively.

"When we first started working together, we would build on what he was saying. If he said one word, we'd try to build from that word to create a sentence." Abrams says it was all very gradual as they moved from words and phrases to complete sentences. She also learned that stamina is an issue when teaching people with TBI "He would get very tired, so he could only do so much."

She had experience working with brain-injured adults. She'd worked previously at the Bloomsburg Reading Clinic where they worked with the Laubach technique that approaches reading with flash cards, word lists and other rote learning tools. Even though she and C.B. had some success with the Laubach approach, Abrams realized that his brain injury was different from others she had worked with in the past. That pushed her to be creative and move the pieces around like a Rubik's Cube until they lined up with his keen memory and receptive language skills. She was learning that no two brain injuries are alike.

Abrams noted that C.B. had difficulty recalling proper nouns. "He could show an understanding about them, but he couldn't say the words." For example, with a little prompting C.B. could talk about some states; he even seemed to know a few things about them. He could share information that he knew about the states but not come up with their names.

She did not find this surprising because dissociation with proper nouns is frequently reported among the brain injured who suffer from aphasia. It also indicates there may be distinct mechanisms in accessing general nouns versus proper nouns. The word "college" may be accessed, for example, but "Notre Dame" just won't come out. Contrarily, there was one proper noun he seemed to get stuck on — Mississippi. He would repeat it constantly until it became something of a running gag.

"My fear was that he was going to perseverate [continually repeat or restate].... He had a great deal of comprehension, but he just kept coming back to that word..." She ultimately concluded that this was a testament to his tenacity. He was trying to meet a challenge that was difficult and frustrating, but he refused to give up on it. "Mississippi" became an alternative to "I don't know." And today it is an inside joke between C.B. and Abrams.

Another example of how he'd clearly understand a concept yet be incapable of conjuring up certain lost words was when Abrams tried to get him to say the word "pharmacy."

"He'd say things like pills, aspirin, bandage, toothpaste," she explained. "He could say all of those words of things you'd find in a pharmacy, but he just couldn't access the word 'pharmacy' itself."

On another occasion, during a conversation with his parents, C.B. was trying to talk about "Troy," a Pennsylvania town not far from their home. In his struggle to come up with that word, other words started coming out. First, he said, "Dallas," followed in short order by the words "football" and "quarterback." Playing for the Dallas Cowboys at the time was Troy Aikman. It was a circuitous route to the word he was trying to say, but C.B. proved to them he recognized the word but couldn't say it. What's more, he found a way to express himself until they figured it out.

The frustrations of aphasia seldom thwarted C.B. Whether he arrived at the word he sought via a musical ditty or by taking a slight detour through his limited vocabulary at the time, C.B. would find a way to say what needed to be said. Another time at a restaurant, where menus remain a barrier, he seemed momentarily stymied when the waitress turned to him to take his order. "I will have a Popeye salad," he proclaimed. He couldn't remember the word "spinach" yet he knew to associate spinach with Popeye.

The brain works in mysterious and miraculous ways, but this inability to recall specific words is a sample of the challenges they would strive to overcome. And C.B. looks back on his tutoring with fondness. Challenges, after all, were what fueled his comeback. "Sylvia [Abrams] made it fun," C.B. says.

Even today it is difficult to quantify how much C.B. actually reads and writes. He can look at an article in the newspaper and understand the gist of what happened, yet he couldn't read the article word-for-word. If he wants to know more than what his limited reading skills provides him, he will push on to read as much as he can, but it is a struggle to put the words together. As for writing, he did a lot of typing for the power-point presentation he uses in his motivational speeches, but he would laboriously copy the sentences as written. He will write things down when he has to, but he is very economical when it comes to dealing with words and numbers. He has a smart phone with the usual phone numbers and reminders, but, whenever possible, he'll hand it to someone else to tap in a new phone number or add something to his calendar.

What he lacks in pure reading efficiency, he makes up for with a comprehension level that is so high he can fill in the content by absorbing key words along the way.

"He could pick up a paper and he would look at it and look at it, and then he might say one or two of the words in front of him," says his mother, "but his brain can't seem to string them together... he can process it, but he can't process it and re-speak it.."

Not surprisingly, C.B. himself cannot really describe how he reads or even explain the extent of his reading skills. Even he seems mystified by how his remapped brain works, but it clearly does what it needs to in order to help C.B. process and understand the world, and written word, around him.

What impressed his father in those early days was C.B.'s conceptual thinking, something Mike realized would be crucial if C.B. were to complete college courses. "You'd see different levels of thought in him," Mike explains, "he would piece things together and make an observation or draw a conclusion.... It really impressed me, because he was really quite infant-like when he started on his own and for quite a while after that, but this thought process showed positive signs"

Before those positive signs, when C.B. was still in his infant-like stage, the challenges seemed daunting at first for Abrams. She worked through those challenges and became one of her student's most ardent admirers: "I did not fully appreciate his greatest gifts – inner strength of character and resilience."

Giving His Dream the Old College Try...

Once he was enrolled in a college program, C.B. started out by retaking some of the courses he had completed at Wilkes University. From there he received his associate's degree cum laude, and he then moved ahead in getting his bachelor's degree. That sounds so simple, written here in a short descriptive paragraph, but it was, something that took eleven years to achieve, taking one course at a time and one after another.

C.B. always has a lot of company when he celebrates his accomplishments. When he fell from that balcony he became part of a much larger family. They are still there for him, and in the summer of 2010 more than 200 people showed up to celebrate C.B.'s bachelor's degree.

After he earned that coveted degree, C.B. wanted to put it to use but there were few job descriptions that applied to him. He approached Abrams to talk over what he might be able to do with his life now that he had a diploma. At Wilkes, he had been on a path to becoming a high school history teacher, but at this point he realized that this might be beyond his capabilities.

"We started to talk about what we could do," Abrams says after he had his hard earned college degree in hand. "We agreed that it can't end here, that there has to be a next thing." Two related goals emerged from their discussions: C.B. wanted to give back and he could help others learn from what he had gone through. He decided his mission was to tell his story to others— either by writing a book, which would require someone to do the writing, and speaking to groups. He was good at talking, so that led naturally to his motivational speaking. And Abrams knew she could help him with the speaking part.

Motivating Others by Telling His Story...

C.B. worked with Abrams to prepare himself for group presentations and motivational talks in which he uses his comeback from TBI to enlighten or inspire. He regularly addresses college students who will be working with the brain injured as therapists, teachers or counselors, as well as at-risk kids who may be inspired by his story. He communicates by speech, but in order to do that, and especially to give group presentations, he needs to recognize key words that keep him on track during his presentations. C.B. is a great ad libber but that occasionally gets him in trouble, because it can distract him, taking him off course. When this happens, he has to find his way back. That might end up as entertaining as his prepared routine but not necessarily as informative. He relies on some slides to help him regain focus

The partnership between C.B. and Abrams resulted in a presentation that includes graphics, photos and taglines. If he chooses to ad lib, or play off somebody in the audience (as he likes to do) he can quickly get back to where he was with a look at the screen. For more informal presentations they devised a card system based on the presentation.

Prior to working with Abrams on his presentation, C.B. had been talking to groups and getting mixed results. Among his stumbling blocks was getting stuck and not knowing where to resume his speech.

Earlier presentations would revolve around a motivational pamphlet, a brace he put on his leg and a poor quality film of a therapy session in which he was being forced to use his right hand to screw off the cap of a bottle. It was a painful exercise with an arm and hand he would never be able to use normally anyway. After attempting this numerous times with his right hand, he just reached out with his left hand and deftly unscrewed the cap.

It may have been an interesting few minutes of footage, but it was a long way to go, and a drain on attention spans, to make a point. The point was that the therapy was pointless if he could accomplish his task with the resources at his disposal. As for the brochure and other items he was passing around, they took his audience's attention from his speech.

"He wants the audience to be comfortable with him," Abrams says. "I tell him, 'All you have to do is open your mouth and start talking and people will get your sense of humor.'" Did you hear the one about this big guy who walks into a room? He's got one eye looking in a different direction, a limp and an arm that doesn't work. That makes him the punch line, and he accepts that. His approach is to put his audience at ease right away, pointing himself out as the elephant in the room and applying a liberal serving of self-deprecation.

C.B, says he has never felt nervous or uncomfortable in front of a group. Like most good speakers, he'd rather work with a large audience than a smaller group, because he prefers to play a crowd. Too few people and it's like trying to get everyone's attention at the breakfast table before they've had their coffee.

His secret? "I'm not all that worried about it. I imagine everyone naked." Pause for effect. "No, not really," he confesses, then falls into one of his signature laughs.

It's not that C.B. has ever needed any rhetorical devices to tell his story. But he's never going to let the elephant in the room go unmentioned.

"I told him 'You know, other people don't just walk up to total strangers on the street and say, 'Hey, I fell from a three-story building,'" says Abrams. "At first, I thought it was almost like an apology, but I don't think it is. I think he just wants people to understand where he is and what he is like. He really wants people to understand, and that's how he does it."

It's not that complicated. His current life started when he fell off that balcony. It was, at first, a tragedy, but he accepts what he is, even revels in it. He truly believes he is lucky and blessed. He is also convinced he has a calling, that he and his family went through all of what they did because there is much more out there beyond mere survival.

When asked about his ease with addressing large crowds, C.B. contemplates the answer, then says: "I've asked myself why this is so easy for me to do, and I think it is really because I have a calling, that I have been called by God to do this."

CHAPTER 12

WHATEVER C.B. WANTS, THEY'LL TRY TO GET

As an acronym, it's something of a stretch. VESID —short for New York's Vocational and Educational Services for Individuals with Disabilities— doesn't even spell out a recognizable word. It sounds more like an insecticide or a pharmaceutical. But Mike Miller is thankful he crossed the border into New York State some two years after C.B.'s accident for a professional seminar presented by two men from VESID. They explained a person-centered model for the lifelong rehabilitation of brain injury survivors.

Mike attended this presentation as part of his exhaustive search to map a path for his son with traumatic brain injury, a very limited vocabulary and a diagnosis from a neuropsychologist as "essentially traumatically illiterate." It had been recommended that C.B. not be placed in any academic environment, because his chances of failure, even with adaptive classroom and study aids, were staggering. Mike, with a firm belief that fear of failure shouldn't hold them back from trying, sought to challenge this recommendation. VESID presented him with a solution.

The VESID model places the brain injury survivor at the center of the plan. The idea is that the survivor himself decides what he wants, and those around him provide a support system established to help him realize his goals. Often, the survivor starts by expressing an interest in the same life goals he had before the accident. Often, the survivor is unable to attain those goals, due to the effects of the injury. But VESID outlines a process that helps the survivors come to this realization on their own so that they are navigating their own course and adapting as new information presents itself.

Mike had grown weary of the constant demands. He felt frustrated, ill-equipped and alone in his mission of assuring his son's independence and sense of purpose. What he heard at that VESID presentation excited him, even though it also created the prospect of additional barriers. To follow this model, he would first have to learn what C.B. himself wanted to do with the rest of his life. It meant setting aside everyone else's expectations and desires, including those of a therapist. The first step would be to find out what C.B. wanted. Then, Mike would strive to establish a structure to help him get it.

What if his goals are unreasonable, clearly doomed to failure?

That's not your decision, a therapist who asked that question was told that day. If the TBI survivor can't do it, he'll be the first to know. And once he realizes that, it's a matter of being there for him and allowing him to revamp his goals. What the survivor needs, according to this model, is a candid appraisal of what lies ahead of him, including all perceived obstacles and hurdles.

Mike must have felt like Moses on Mount Sinai, receiving the word that he immediately recognized as a gateway leading to the Promised Land. Like Moses, he also recognized there would be trials and hardships before journey's end. And he knew that he was genuinely excited, if not giddy, at the prospect of what this approach could mean for C.B.

One reason this struck such a responsive chord was that it captured the approach Mike and Sharon Miller had used to raise their children. They always encouraged them to pursue what they found interesting and challenging. If that pursuit ended in disappointment—not making a sports team or falling short of reaping some academic honor, for instance—Mike and Sharon were there to support them. Failure, if that was how you described it, was a learning experience, and just because you didn't succeed as you might have hoped, it doesn't mean you didn't learn something valuable along the way. Why should it not be the same for someone with traumatic brain injury?

One key to this strategy, as Mike learned in the presentation, was to form a team who could guide the survivor along the way. This team typically comprised of professionals who probably wouldn't be a resource available to Mike back in rural Pennsylvania. Mike quickly discerned that his resource, as it had been in transporting C.B. to and from outpatient therapy and fulfilling other special needs, would have to be volunteers.

Mike describes his conflicting emotions after attending the seminar: "As I drove home, and even throughout the next day, this model kept buzzing through my mind. I was excited with the concept but anxious about how to implement it. The VESID people had paid staff and assistance. I had nothing. How could I create an atmosphere where we could not only ask C.B. the question about his future, but be able to help him move toward it?

"The anxious feeling was one that I had quite often after C.B.'s accident. I seemed to constantly be in a position where I could see what had to happen but felt that I was the only one who could make it happen. Sometimes the things that had to be done were way beyond my capabilities, yet I had to find a way to make them happen. In the case of the VESID approach, how could I set things up so that no matter what C.B.'s answers were when asked what he wants or needs to do, I could offer him at least a chance of attaining it?"

Mike already had a good guess of what C.B. would tell him he wanted most: to regain his driver's license and to go back to college and finish his degree. C.B. had planned to be a history teacher when he was attending Wilkes, but he had all the requisite tools then, including an above-average IQ and the ability to read and write.

The driver's license would seem to be the easiest of these goals to achieve. He had lost it in the wake of his accident, probably because doctors were required to notify the Pennsylvania Department of Transportation (PennDOT) of his brain injury. Then there was the seizure he had the day after the accident— the only one he ever had. Seizures were a possible consequence of his injuries. The strategy employed by the neurosurgeon on the night of C.B.'s accident was to utilize a drug-induced coma at a relatively light level and see if he would have any seizures. Then, if he did, the dose would be increased in phases until the seizures stopped. When Dr. Sedor took over supervising C.B.'s treatment he opted to put him in a deep drug-induced coma to eliminate the possibility of seizures. It was a strategy that worked. C.B. never had another seizure in all the years that ensued.

An educational advisory team, as the VESID model dictated, was subsequently convened to formulate a game plan. C.B. not only attended these planning sessions, he worked with his father to develop an agenda for them. At first, there seemed to be reluctance on the part of team members to express opinions. Mike, sensing they lacked understanding of how someone with a severe brain injury might function, reviewed the model, then asked for a show of hands from anyone with prior experience dealing with brain injury survivors.

Only one hand shot up—C.B.'s. The room erupted in laughter, which cleared the air for a candid discussion.

With his vocabulary still very limited, C.B. explained that he did not feel capable of going directly to a college classroom; he thought he should start slowly. A strategy soon evolved that started with C.B. observing a high school class taught by one of his favorite former teachers. From there, he would sit in on other high school courses, then audit college-level courses to get a feel for what lay ahead. C.B. would make the choices and the team would be there to monitor his progress and advise him along the way.

While all of this was going on, Mike was attempting to learn of special services available through Social Security's disability benefits. It provided the opportunity to document C.B.'s brain injury and the inherent challenges it presented. Naturally, it could open the door for benefits they might not otherwise be able to afford. The chief purpose was trying to understand just what the benefits were and how and where C.B. might qualify. It would also mean a series of tortuous confrontations with a caseworker who, in Mike's words, "acted like she thought we were trying to cheat the government (or perhaps her personally) out of all their money."

It turned out to be an extremely adversarial relationship, with Mike dreading each meeting with the caseworker. At the time, it seemed to be the only course he could take, and he tried every tactic he could think of to ingratiate himself to the civil servant. She was, in fact, less of a servant than a dictator who knew she was in complete control. They got off to a rocky start when she took issue with Mike, as C.B.'s power of attorney, using his son's savings account to keep record of funds needed to pay ongoing bills, such as rehabilitation expenses and special driver's training. It apparently created a situation where an account in C.B.'s name averaged over the allowable amount and threatened to disqualify him for disability benefits. Even though the total bills exceeded the amount in the account, he was reprimanded and ordered to pay back benefits received to that point.

Because he was not learning anything, other than what he was supposedly doing wrong, Mike, as noted before, set about doing his own exhaustive study of Social Security regulations and offerings. The breaking point came when he was reprimanded and essentially accused of wrongdoing for setting up a Supplemental Needs Trust, which, as his attorney had advised, would help take care of C.B.'s future financial needs without affecting his eligibility for Social Security benefits. It was basically a repository for money coming out of their liability settlement.

"The problem arose when I informed our Social Security caseworker of it," Mike recalls of an exchange that would end with him walking out of her office in complete frustration. "She again tried to berate me and informed me that we could not do this. She also made it perfectly clear that she would make me pay for the stupid thing that we had done."

This led to seeking advice from a friend who was a manager in another Social Security office, who suggested transferring their case to the regional office in Williamsport, PA. Furthermore, Mike was advised that he could file a complaint against the abusive caseworker. He did take his business elsewhere in the Social Security hierarchy, where the issue was promptly resolved, and continues to do so today. And though he believed filing a complaint was warranted, "I did not have time or energy enough to get involved in a bureaucratic process."

Time and energy only go so far— even for the likes of Mike Miller.

Simpler Goal Becomes Complicated...

What appeared to be a simple start would become immensely complicated before C.B. would actually be enrolled as a college student. The supposedly easy goal of reclaiming his driver's license proved to be more of an ordeal than anticipated. PennDOT's standard reinstatement procedure when dealing with reported seizures was to rely on a letter from an attending physician, stating that the prospective driver had been seizure-free for a prescribed period of time. As for his associated disabilities, there were adaptive measures available that would allow him to drive without a functioning right arm and right leg.

"I did not want him behind the wheel until he could be checked out and found to be safe," was Mike's mindset at the time. Anyone who drives may find himself in harm's way. Life had to be lived, not avoided, if C.B. were to complete his comeback. Staffers at Heinz pointed them to a company where driving efficiency was evaluated using special equipment in training vehicles.

The other factor was his damaged left eye, which had been realigned through a series of multiple surgeries, both constructive and cosmetic. They made an appointment for testing with an ophthalmologist. With eyeglasses, C.B. did not seem to have any significant sight issues. That scenario changed on the day of the eye exam. The doctor informed them, after testing, that C.B. seemed to have lost all of his peripheral vision, meaning there was little chance he'd ever get behind the wheel of a car again.

"As he said this I felt like he was punching me in the stomach as hard as he could," Mike remembers. "It really took the wind right out of me."

Then Mike started second-guessing his strategy, setting his son up to fail and, more critically, allowing him to absorb another disappointment. Perhaps he had let C.B. down by not following his paternal instinct to protect him from further trauma after all he had been through.

It was C.B.'s response that saved him from settling into self-doubt about the direction he had chosen to take. As important as driving seemed to be, C.B. took the setback quite nonchalantly. It was Mike who was most discouraged by the sting of failure. C.B. seemed to take it in stride.

"He was the one who actually supported me and helped me to find the strength to stick with our person-directed plan," Mike says of that day.

The driver's license effort was put on hold—that is, until Mike met again with the VESID duo and told them about the setback. They were sympathetic to his instinct as a father wanting to protect his son, but they took issue with his decision to back off and leave it at that.

"After I told them about the experience and my disappointment, there first question was 'What did you do about this?' I answered that I tried to distract C.B. by focusing him on his return to the classroom. At this point they admonished me, telling me that I should not give up so easily. I should have pursued the licensing agency in Pennsylvania to see if, indeed, the loss of peripheral vision would prevent him from getting his license back. The only way to do that was to re-start the effort to have him evaluated and tested."

As the old saying goes, that was to be easier said than done. It eventually proved to be feasible, even if painfully slow. The first step would be to cut through an undergrowth of red tape presented by PennDOT. PennDOT apparently did not have a procedure for issuing a learner's permit to someone who already had a driver's license. Typically, it would be a case of simply re-issuing the license once PennDOT had received a physician's approval and accompanying paperwork.

"PennDOT seemed to be so confused that over the period of time it took us to get his learner's permit, we received instructions for him to report for a driver's exam, a separate letter threatening to suspend his already suspended license (we were eventually told that we received this because it was the only letter that the computer could generate) and an opportunity to actually renew his old license without any exam," explains Mike.

They could have taken the easy way out by pursuing the latter option, and then have him undergo driver's training before allowing him on the road. But what Mike really needed was assurance from an objective party that C.B. would be a safe driver with no obscure liability issues. That would have to be the people in the licensing arm of PennDOT. What followed was a comedy of misadventures in the pursuit of the appropriate department, until Mike finally made contact with a real person in Harrisburg who actually understood the dilemma.

From there it was a few more phone calls and letters and C.B.'s learning permit arrived one day in the mail. Now he could begin his driver's training with a company experienced in working with people with challenges, and that required a 70-mile drive each way. It seemed a minor inconvenience in light of the circuitous route to get there. In the meantime, since the earlier eye exam, there had been additional surgery on his left eye to deal with double-vision. This subsequently resulted in follow-up testing and the revelation that his peripheral vision was now within the normal range.

And, yes, he would pass his driver's exam with flying colors. Adaptive equipment in his vehicle would include a left-footed gas pedal, a steering wheel attachment, known, unfortunately, as a "suicide knob," and special rearview mirror insets to allow better peripheral and distance sightlines.

Being able to drive would prove to be a tremendous boost to his independence. It was, in hindsight, a tremendous accomplishment, and a huge motivation to move ahead with his next goal— one that would take more than a decade to achieve.

"He had three challenges that made this picture hard to imagine," Mike said of C.B.'s successful retrieval of his driving privileges. "One was his stamina, a symptom that is common in almost every person who has suffered a traumatic brain injury. Another is his aphasia, which made reading and writing very difficult for him. Then there were his physical challenges, the loss of effective use of his right arm and leg."

At the same time the Millers were working towards getting C.B. back behind the wheel as an independent driver, they were seeking ways to help him make strides towards his goal of obtaining a college degree. Over the course of a couple of years, they would bring together a group of individuals to serve as C.B.'s educational advisory team. This team would help position C.B. to start taking college courses in earnest. And then it would be one course at a time, one each semester, for eleven years. Leading up to that he had been auditing high school classes, and receiving literacy tutoring from two volunteers.

It seemed as if they had embarked on a new phase of C.B.'s comeback.

"We had come through the period where we could mourn the loss of C.B. as we knew him before," is how his father viewed it. "Now we were at a point where we could rejoice in learning who C.B. was becoming after the accident."

Facing the Most Demanding Goal...

There would be little time for rejoicing or even congratulatory pats on the back as the Millers continued their quests. Rehabilitation had led to a phase of re-education and rediscovery. It was time to meet the most demanding goal of all —a college degree.

This required Mike to continue what had brought them this far. He researched and questioned, hoping to find the best way to help C.B. reach this goal. And he overcame moments of doubt and setback and lack of resources. He pushed ahead, paving the way for C.B. to move forward with his new life.

In consulting with members of C.B.'s educational advisory team, Mike learned about a series of neuropsychological tests called the Woodcock-Johnson Psycho-Educational Battery. These tests were used to assess cognitive abilities, which seemed a logical, if not critical step to get C.B. back into a college classroom.

Mike regarded it as another tool they could use to get C.B. where they wanted him to go. Perhaps it would backfire but by now, he learned that C.B. could handle such setbacks and his attitude seemed to be that today's failure would merely be tomorrow's challenge. If C.B. was ever worried about failure, he never showed it.

The neuropsychologist asked to perform the tests seemed hesitant to deal with a father who was neither an educator nor seemingly conversant in the field of education. Typically a request for this battery of tests would come from someone directly involved and employed in education. There was also a significant cost. The testing cost a minimum of $1,200, and Mike suspected the specialist was dubious about his ability to pay out of pocket. However, when Mike mentioned that a state-run agency might pay for it through a program in which C.B. was already involved, there was a marked change in attitude, and the neuropsychologist agreed to administer the tests.

The state-run agency offering to foot the bill for the tests was the Office of Vocational Rehabilitation. OVR helps people with disabilities return to the work place. At the time C.B. was trying to return to college, OVR did not have a lot of experience helping persons with traumatic brain injury. C.B. presented OVR with an opportunity to learn about a new set of needs.

Eventually, after testing and auditing and easing back into the educational process, more than five years after a plunge from a balcony would render the left side of his brain virtually nonfunctional, C.B. found himself back in a college classroom. Through a Weekender program offered by Keystone College, C.B. began to earn college credits in his hometown. It took him five years to receive an associate's degree. Then in another six years, he would realize his goal and graduate with a bachelor's degree.

Between earning the two diplomas, C.B. decided on his own he would not pursue his original goal of being a history teacher. As Mike Miller had been advised, C.B. would be the first to know if he needed to change his goals. Based on career and psychological evaluations, as well as Keystone's degree offerings on the program, he himself would ultimately decide to major in business administration and a minor in human resources management.

"I think he realized his aphasia would hold him back as a teacher in the classroom," says his father who believes C.B. was concerned that he wouldn't be able to communicate what he needed to his students. "He might be able to do that today, the way he has progressed. But we couldn't have foreseen that back then, while he was taking courses toward a degree. Since them, we've learned kids relate really well to him."

In 2010, sixteen years after the fall, the Millers held a gathering to celebrate C.B.'s graduation from Keystone College. While the degree might not lead him directly to a job and a career, at least not in the traditional sense, it was the realization of a hard-earned goal. And it would become part of the inspiring success story that C.B. shared with others as a motivational speaker. It also represented the continuation of a developing credo: "When friends help, miracles happen." The Millers wanted all to know that no matter what role each person played in allowing C.B. to achieve this milestone, it was an important one. The journey was —and still is— truly about taking one small step at a time, and being surrounded by a supportive community, friends and family as each step is taken.

Labeling C.B.'s academic accomplishment as hard earned would be an understatement. Whereas a typical student could take notes and dedicate a few hours of weekly study to stay on top of the subject matter, C.B. would require numerous hours of his time, as well as his father's, to have the study material at his disposal. Before he even started a class, it was essential to meet with the instructor to acquaint him or her with C.B.'s disability, the constraints of his functional literacy and his special needs. Those needs, of course, would revolve around oral learning and repetition. It wasn't the job of instructors to do any of this, but their understanding and cooperation were imperative. This meeting also proactively addressed potential challenges that might lie ahead in classroom instruction.

Here's what had to be done for just one class: C.B. would use a tape recorder to record all lectures, comments and instructions. His memory was outstanding, so there was a learning process in the classroom itself. That was just the beginning. The recordings would be transcribed by his father so that C.B. could listen to it to refresh his memory. After getting the lesson on paper, Mike would then go over the material with C.B., as well as any textbook assignments, by drilling repeatedly. For every hour in the classroom, there were dozens of hours between the two of them to keep up with the assignments and be test ready. Tests, of course, would be administered and answered orally.

A huge break for both father and son came when Mike discovered a technological aid. It is the Kurzweil Reader, and it became C.B.'s constant study companion. The taped lessons would still have to be transcribed, but once printed the Kurzweil Reader could take over. It scans any text, whether typed, electronic or on the web, and reads it aloud as directed, word by word. This allows for visual reinforcement along with the oral reading. The software may even be used for written tests, assignments and worksheets.

That meant C.B. could work and study without his father's assistance, using just his computer and software. He eventually relieved his father's burden even more when he, on his own, availed himself of tutoring services offered by the college.

"I went to my parents and asked them if I could do this," says C.B. of tutors provided by Keystone. "They thought it was a good idea, and it worked out great."

Working with the tutors and being more independently directed in his studies also boosted C.B.'s confidence and made him less reliant on his father, who was also still working full-time and dealing with C.B.'s legal, medical, vocational and financial issues.

"Dad would never say it was too much. That's not him. He's going to keep pushing and pushing, doing what he has to do and whatever it takes to get it done," C.B. says with admiration.

C.B. was walking a path of transition from rehabilitation to education. Rehabilitation addresses rediscovering what you knew in the past. Education is about learning something new. It was never clear when this transition occurred or where the path might lead. What mattered most was that C.B. be enabled and empowered to continue along the path.

As is often the case, red tape and burrowing through the bureaucracy proved to be the greatest hurdles in keeping C.B.'s comeback on track. It can't be overstated on any of the fronts, whether it was making the tough decisions in seeking the civil relief that would give him a shot at lifelong self-reliance or meeting more immediate goals. Detailing all the moves and countermoves that allowed C.B. to earn a college degree alone would be enough for a book in itself—a primer, if you will, of hits and misses.

"Our goal was not to focus on getting high grades," Mike says of the philosophy that eventually evolved as they worked toward C.B.'s goal of earning his degree. "It was more about improving the cognitive abilities and knowledge level through the classroom experience."

Dual Purposes: Learning and Thinking...

Educators, however, were often not on the same page as Mike, and he soon came to realize that he was asking them to venture into foreign territory—accommodating the brain injured in the pursuit of higher education. He recalls meeting with the director of one college program that was highly acclaimed in the disability community. The administrator was apparently accustomed to and experienced in providing remedies and adaptive measures for physical disabilities in the classroom, but the questions he was being asked by Mike centered on cognitive or learning supports. The director's level of agitation clearly increased until he finally blurted out: "Mr. Miller, we are in the business of education, not rehabilitation."

It struck Mike that this professional was overlooking a fundamental truth: that education is learning, and learning comes in various forms.

Mike's expectations for his disabled son were the same as those he would hold were C.B. not thwarted by brain injury. He sought an opportunity for C.B. to learn through understanding and developing thinking skills. He did not want an environment where "a professor imparted his knowledge on the lowly student," treating him like a repository primed to regurgitate information with minimal processing.

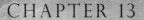

CHAPTER 13

MAKING A DIFFERENCE BY GIVING BACK

The Center for Disease Control and Prevention (CDC) reports that about 2.5 million people a year are treated in emergency rooms, hospitalized or die from a traumatic brain injury. Over 50,000 of them die. Roughly 280,000 of the others require hospitalization, and often surgery, to survive.

That leaves about 2.2 million individuals, some 88 percent of those who sustain a TBI each year, who never get further than the emergency room. They are treated and released, with the consequences of the brain injury often remaining a mystery. The effects of treating and releasing these individuals are largely unknown. It's difficult to conclude if their brain injury leaves them more susceptible to illness or perhaps causes changes in behavior.

TBI is recognized as a prolific killer, or at least a formidable accomplice in many deaths in the United States. It is a contributing factor in a third of all injury-related deaths in the U.S. each year. The

CDC describes TBI as a "public health problem" and a leading cause of death and disability in the U.S.

In 2010, the CDC estimated that more than 5.3 million people in the U.S. were living with a long-term disability due to a TBI, and that roughly 80,000 people joined their ranks each year. With numbers like these, it becomes clear that there is a sizable segment of the U.S. population that is coping with life after TBI. Many of them are unable to function independently.

C.B. Miller is both a perfect example of a TBI survivor and a rare case. Considering the severity of his injury, he is incredibly fortunate. People who fall from third-story balconies, if they survive at all, often end up in nursing care homes. C.B. has worked hard to defy the odds, not just of surviving, but thriving after suffering a TBI.

The Nature of Brain Injuries

The brain is a uniquely protected organ. The outermost layer of protection is provided by skull and facial bones. Eight bones in the skull and fourteen bones in the face together provide a first line of defense to outside forces. Within that fortress lies another layer of protection—the cerebrospinal fluid (CSF). The brain is essentially suspended in CSF, which cushions the vital organ and acts as a shock absorber, allowing for some leeway before the brain bumps against the skull. The next line of defense is provided by three membranes collectively called the meninges. The outermost layer, known as the dura, is thick and tough and can restrict movement of the brain. The middle layer of the meninges is the arachnoid, and the innermost layer is the pia mater. From skull to pia, the body provides many layers that serve as a safeguard to the brain. But even the best safeguards can't protect against everything. .

The most common injuries to the brain—concussions and mild TBI —are caused by a jolt, blow or collision that causes the brain to slam against the inside of the skull. This may cause a bruising of the brain tissue known as a contusion with symptoms that include some swelling and broken blood vessels. If significant bleeding occurs from one or more of these broken vessels, blood may pool and form a hematoma. A hematoma is more insidious because it may occur deeper in the brain.

These common types of injuries may cause increased pressure on the brain, which can cause swelling of an organ that has little room to expand inside its protective skull. The brain essentially harms itself by pushing against bone. In the worst-case scenario, this could lead to herniation, or rupture of the brain tissue with fatal consequences. More often it will be remembered only as a headache, grogginess or temporary memory loss. Unfortunately, many of these mild injuries go untreated. A concussion is considered a form of mild TBI, but it still may be life-altering, disease accelerating and, sadly, often undiagnosed.

TBI is the leading cause of death among infants and children under the age of five. There is a high incidence of TBI among teens and young adults due to automobile accidents and war casualties. People age 75 and older are the most highly represented age group in terms of TBI-related hospitalizations and deaths, reports the U.S. Department of Health and Human Services. People 65 and older are most likely to fall. Falls can cause trauma to the brain— injuries from which a younger person would more likely recover.

Brain injury can strike at any age, and it does. According to North American Brain Injury Society, traumatic brain injury is the leading cause of death and disability around the world. It is hard to believe that so little attention is paid to it, because we all probably know someone with TBI... even if we don't realize it.

Most of the statistics published about TBI pertain to people initially treated in hospital emergency rooms. They do not include those who opt instead to see their primary care physicians or, as is too often the case, do not seek treatment at all. In a 2009 report, the Brain Injury Association of America maintained that there is a large number of people (as few as 1.6 million and as many as 3.8 million) who sustain sports-related concussions each year and fail to seek immediate attention.

While determining how many people suffer a mild traumatic brain injury might involve a guessing game because not all of those cases are reported, severe traumatic brain injury is another story. When an incident leads to trauma treated at the hospital, those cases can be documented. Where the guessing game applies in those instances is something quite different. It applies when determining what effects a massive destruction of brain cells might have, or predicting the prospects of recovery and rehabilitation.

Setting Some Lofty Standards...

Regarding his TBI as a challenge that must be met rather than an inevitable handicap to work around, the Millers were positioning C.B. for recovery far exceeding that which was the accepted rehabilitation goal for traumatic brain injury in 1994. They set their sights on the long-term yet focused on the here-and-now, addressing immediate needs that enabled C.B. to step into a considerably brighter future than anyone might have predicted for him in the immediate days after his tragic fall.

"He just set the standards so high," Sharon Miller says of the course her husband chose to take with C.B. Somewhere along the road to learning all he could to help the way for C.B.'s comeback, Mike Miller became an advocate for a lot of people affected by brain injury. In fact, he likely played a crucial role in saving other families from many of the things he and his family went through.

Through his proactive approach to his son's brain injury, Mike became actively involved with the Brain Injury Association of Pennsylvania. He has served as vice president, as well as chairing the Pennsylvania Department of Health's TBI Advisory Board. In addition, he chairs a group called the Pennsylvania Brain Injury Coalition, which leads a cooperative effort involving the Brain Injury Association of Pennsylvania, the Acquired Brain Injury Network of Pennsylvania and the Rehabilitation and Community Providers Association. .

While his experiences dealing with C.B.'s TBI drew Mike to this volunteer service initially, the focus of his advocacy has evolved. Today, a good portion of his work relates to what many people regard as the least traumatic brain injury— the concussion. Historically, concussions have not been considered to be TBI. While the distinction between "concussion" and "mild TBI" might seem to be a matter of semantics, it can be significant in terms of diagnosis, treatment and insurance coverage for the injured. The distinction also plays out in special education services after a brain injury. This is one reason why the Brain Injury Association of America is calling for all of them to be labeled brain injury for the sake of both treatment and vocational rehabilitation.

Before the accident, one of C.B.'s teammates at Wilkes was the Colonels' quarterback, Damon "Boo" Perry, who introduced him to brain injury of a different sort. By the time he finished his four years as a starter at Wilkes, Perry had suffered multiple concussions. The first was as a junior in high school. As a freshman at Wilkes, Perry took a hit in the opening quarter while playing Widener.

"I basically played the whole game on automatic pilot. I do not remember how we scored or what the score was. I was still calling plays and running plays," Perry recalls. "There were 10 minutes to go in the game and they bring in a play. I just looked at them and said, 'I don't know what that is.' That's when they figured it out."

He was standing on the sidelines next to one of the offensive linemen, C.B. Miller.

"I asked C.B., 'Who's winning?' I must have asked him a dozen times, and he'd say, 'Boo, it's 14-14.' A minute later I'd ask him again."

C.B. remembers that his brother, the doctor, was in the stands and upset after the game because nobody had so much as examined Perry, let alone taken him to the hospital. When they did, it was hours later. It was diagnosed as a concussion, and Perry sat out the last two games of the season and wore a special padded helmet in the following seasons.

In terms of attitudes toward concussions, the Wilkes coaches showed more sensitivity than others might have back in 1994 by keeping

Perry off the field for the remainder of his inaugural season there. It was a time when kids, playing both high school and college, routinely went back into the game after incurring concussions. Perry himself would sustain another concussion on the field before leaving Wilkes.

Today, the father of two daughters, Perry is one of the lucky ones. He's missing a few scenes from his past, events he doesn't remember, but that was from the shroud of forgetfulness around the time of the concussion itself. The only after effect he can attribute to his concussions is a sensitively to loud noises and abrasive sounds like static on the radio.

"That kind of stuff just drives me up the wall," he confesses. "I know I dodged a bullet, I guess you'd say, because you read about players going back into the game after a concussion and then they go home and have a seizure... or worse."

This was more than a year before C.B. fell off that balcony. At the time, it was unlikely that the Millers or Perry thought much of it. In retrospect, however, the story has taken on new meaning. As Mike got more involved in issues associated with TBI, he became cognizant of the lack of awareness most people have about mild TBI and concussions. And his advocacy would eventually turn to address this very issue.

November 14, 2011, was a date for the record books, and a memorable one for Mike. On that day, Pennsylvania Governor Tom Corbett signed a bill known as Safety in Youth Sports Act, "establishing standards for managing concussions and traumatic brain injuries to student athletes; assigning duties to the Department of Health and the Department of Education; and imposing penalties." As Chairman of the Pennsylvania Brain Injury Coalition at that time, Mike had been instrumental in moving that forward. It was something he worked on for four years.

The Act went into effect in June of 2012, requiring all students and their parents to sign a document that states they have been given and reviewed information on concussions. Passing the Act was clearly the right thing to do, but getting it to reach the legislature required constant and aggressive advocacy —an almost daily vigilance. And it didn't make it through the first time it was up for consideration. Pennsylvania governing bodies took some convincing, even though more than half of the states had already passed such legislation to protect their high school athletes. When it did pass, however, it passed unanimously in both chambers of the Pennsylvania legislature, a point noted by the governor in his statement at the signing ceremony.

Thanks to many similar bills being passed throughout the U.S., the days are gone when coaches passed smelling salts or asked how many fingers they were holding up before letting athletes back into the game. The new set of criteria in the state of Pennsylvania requires that before an athlete can return to play, she/he must have a signed authorization from a medical professional trained in the area of concussions. As long as coaches follow the letter of the law, they are protected from being sued. It seems fitting that the Vice President of the Brain Injury Association of Pennsylvania and chief advocate of the so-called high school concussion bill made the formal response on the association's behalf when the governor signed the bill into law:

"The Brain Injury Association of Pennsylvania is proud to have played a part with the coalition that has worked on the passage of this important piece of legislation. This legislation will help to insure the safety of the many student athletes in Pennsylvania and prevent catastrophic losses from concussion. The Association looks forward to working with the Pennsylvania Athletic Trainers Society and the Pennsylvania School Board Association in assisting the more than 500 Pennsylvania school districts to implement programs to fulfill the requirements of this legislation."

That statement was issued by Mike Miller.

People often associate concussions with a bump, blow or jolt directly to the head. But concussions can also occur from a blow to the body that causes the head to move rapidly back and forth. Concussions, if not appropriately treated, can permanently disrupt the way the brain normally works. They can result in dizziness, nausea, double vision, headache, confusion and problems with balance, concentration or memory. With appropriate care, many of these symptoms may be resolved, but in some athletes, they may persist. Even a "ding" or a bump on the head can be serious and can result in a long-term or lifelong disability. Baseline neurocognitive testing on a student athlete before the sports season is an important tool for their protection, the foundation that must be laid to detect brain injury.

The bottom line is that a concussion is a brain injury, and the educational effort in Pennsylvania is now inclusive with kids, parents and schools. Mike Miller was instrumental in that— something good that came from C.B.'s brain injury.

Boo Perry has nothing but praise for what he calls Mike Miller's crusade: "What he has helped to get done should have been done a long time ago."

Dr. Michael Raymond knows something about brain injury, whether it is TBI or concussions. He, too, played a role in C.B. Miller's recovery when he was the head of the Brain Injury Team at the Heinz Rehab Hospital in Wilkes-Barre. He pointed out in an essay that so-called minor brain injury may have major consequences, reaffirming something he has stressed previously:

"The potential cumulative effects of multiple concussions over time (prior to the brain fully recovering from an initial concussion) can be devastating. The worst scenario is permanent brain damage or even death; this is well documented in the clinical literature."

That makes it even clearer that Perry, with his multiple concussions starting as an adolescent, has lived a charmed life in the two decades following his playing days. He was not protected, as young athletes are today by programs such as the Safety in Youth Sports Act, but he understands he was just a product of the times.

"I have no animosity toward anyone, even if I look back and feel that I was actually brain injured then," he says. "With what we know today, I wouldn't want anybody's kid to take the chances I probably took."

As Dr. Raymond has noted in support of the high school concussion bill, we need to get over what he called "prehistoric sayings" that suggest, as they did in the sports lives of anyone over the age of thirty, that you've got to get back in the game no matter what. "No pain, no gain," takes on new meaning when you're talking about someone with a brain injury standing on the sideline itching to return to the fray.

Mike Miller has made a difference, for his son, for his local community and even for his home state of Pennsylvania. Now his son who has come back so far wants to make a difference, too. His brain injury motivated his father to greater things. Now C.B. has to do the same for himself.

A Near Disaster on a Fateful Day...

July 21, 2005 was eleven years to the day after his fall from the balcony. In fact, it was because of the anniversary date that C.B. was driving to Wilkes-Barre on scenic Route 6. It had become an annual pilgrimage for him, an observation of his re-birth and to visit his saviors at Heinz and elsewhere.

Rounding a curve, something happened that caused C.B.'s Chevy Blazer to roll three times. Emergency volunteers from nearby Wysox and Wyalusing extricated him from the wreckage, and C.B. was life-flighted to the Robert Packer Hospital in Sayre.

Mike and Sharon Miller were in Harrisburg at a meeting of the TBI Advisory Board, when they got the call on their cell phone. Sharon answered and the woman on the other end said she was from the Robert Packer and that their son, Christopher, had been in a motor vehicle accident. She was stunned in disbelief and, just as on that night eleven years before, handed the phone to her husband.

"I went over to Mike and said, 'You've got to take this. They've got to have something wrong. It can't be C.B. He's supposed to be in Wilkes-Barre'... I had to be in denial, I was thinking it just can't be."

But it was.

C.B. sustained a mild concussion from the accident, injured his fifth vertebrae and sustained an impingement to his left shoulder. He was released in a week and wore a neck collar for about three months as a reminder of his anniversary day.

"His guardian angel is up there with her hands on her hips just shaking her head," says his mother, who couldn't help but notice what seemed to be an accelerated improvement in his communication skills over the ensuing months. "Sometimes I wondered if it jarred something. There were times when he even seemed sharper..."

That might not be a valid medical opinion, but there is something to be said for a mother's intuition.

CHAPTER 14

WELCOME TO THE WORLD OF THE BLESSED

While dining out with his family one evening, C.B. took note of another restaurant patron. Something about the middle-aged man's appearance and behavior felt familiar. His expression, the way he moved... it caught C.B.'s keen attention. Stepping outside for a cigarette break, C.B. was able to talk to this stranger who somehow seemed familiar.

In his usual direct fashion, C.B. asked the stranger point-blank: "Are you brain injured?" Upon receiving a casual confirmation of his suspicion, C.B. belatedly realized his question may have seemed brazen, possibly even offensive, and quickly apologized for getting too personal then revealed himself as a TBI survivor. The fellow waved off the apology with an understanding smile.

"I never mind being asked by one of the blessed," he said to C.B.

Brain injury is a blessing. For those who have come back from traumatic brain injury to live and love, they savor what they regard as not just a second chance, but a rebirth. C.B. Miller, like his newfound friend in the restaurant, feels this way.

C.B. does not think of his accident, which so dramatically changed the course of his young life, as a tragic event. C.B. sees himself as one of the fortunate few who defied the odds. He even pays homage to the place where one life ended and another began.

"I always go to see where I got hurt because it is very, very calming," he says. "That building was the start of my life. That's where I got hurt. That's where I started over."

The porch he fell from has been torn down.

While his life may have started with that tragic fall in 1994, some relationships ended with it. Whether because of guilt or the need for separation after a traumatic event, some friendships drifted away. C.B. is a little puzzled by that, but he seems to understand that everyone has to move on in his or her own way.

It was tough on everyone. One of his old roommates was at that party, standing near C.B. when he took the plunge. When this roommate visited C.B. in the hospital soon after the accident, C.B.'s mother noticed he was upset as he left. She followed him to see what was wrong. "He told me that he should have stopped C.B. from falling," Sharon recalls. "I could see how upset he was at the thought of missing an opportunity to prevent C.B.'s fall... I pulled him in for a hug and told him there was no way he could have stopped him, and that even if he'd tried, he'd have fallen too."

Survivor guilt can sometimes be more painful and enduring than massive injuries. C.B. cannot remember the fall and the three months following. His new memories start somewhere around the time he started rehab in the fall of 1994. Months are missing from his memory. He can't recall the pain he felt upon impact or the aches endured while recovering in I.C.U. In some strange way, the brain seems to have protected him from the agony of remembering those moments. Those who were with C.B. at the time of the fall, they can remember it all. They remember it clearly. The injured brain might protect itself from recalling trauma. The healthy mind, however, does not.

As is the case with most people, C.B. has lost some friends over the course of time. It happens—life tends to separate people as the years pass. In C.B.'s case, however, traumatic brain injury has played a role in his enduring friendships. It changed the chemistry in his relationships with old friends. He's not the guy they assumed he'd become when they were pals in high school. Once on similar trajectories involving college and careers, their paths diverged on that fateful night. His high school friends are now well into careers, raising families and dealing with more typical life experiences most of us face. C.B., however belongs to a rare demographic. He's a TBI survivor.

"C.B. no longer grieves and I don't think his parents do either," says Sylvia Abrams, C.B.'s speech teacher and career guide. His grieving has never been voiced, leaving one to wonder if it ever happened or, like his anger, was resolved during the time he was basically silenced by the aphasia."

When he walks up to strangers and introduces himself by telling them that his name is C.B. Miller and he fell forty-two feet from a balcony back in 1994, he is not explaining why he looks or acts the way he does. He is sharing his story of comeback, hoping to reach others and tell them everything's going to be okay, no matter how difficult life might seem at times.

For some, C.B.'s immediate ease with strangers is worrisome. "I think he is, to a fault, too forward," says his brother Michael. "This is probably at least partly due to injuries to his frontal lobe. He lacks the social grace of allowing personal space and leaving people alone. He'll talk to anybody... which is a good and bad thing."

Michael has always feared C.B. would be subject to doing stuff people told him to do. That hasn't really happened. He doesn't seem to be a follower. He usually has a plan, a schedule, and he tends to stick to it. His brother confesses surprise that, despite this bold nature, he's never really been turned away: "It's wild when you think about it. I've never seen anybody say, 'Get away from me pal,' or had that kind of reaction."

C.B. likes to joke around. He thinks he jokes more in this life than he did in the first one, but some might beg to differ. "And if I don't know somebody I probably joke more." It's that self-effacing Miller thing, as his brother likes to call it.

C.B. has faced ridicule and strangers making fun of him. How does he handle that? "I just wait for him to be done and go the other way. I can't fight, because I'm probably going to be in trouble. Only got one arm that works and I'm easy to knock off my feet," he says, with a twinkle in his eye.

"People can be very judgmental just listening to him talk and looking at him, but he doesn't let that stop him," says his sister, Maurie. "Eventually they see past the appearance and impaired speech patterns, and most people grow to love him."

Still Figuring Out the Spiritual Part...

C.B. appreciates any display of love or affection, even when he doesn't visibly show it. He remains a loyal follower of his high school sports teams. The Towanda football and baseball players especially have come to expect to see him at their games. A few years after his accident, C.B. missed a big game because of a doctor's appointment. He was still living with his parents, and after returning home, he was taking a shower when the doorbell rang.

His mother answered the door to find one of the baseball players standing on her stoop and a school bus parked on the street behind him. She explained that C.B. was in the shower. The athlete dutifully shared the news with the team by shouting it over his shoulder, towards the bus. "I don't care if he has to come out in a towel," the coach shouted back. "Tell him to get out here!"

When C.B. finally appeared at the door (the team waited patiently while he dressed), he was greeted with a large cheer from the high school athletes on that bus. The team wanted to share the news of their win with one of their biggest and most loyal fans, and to let him know that they'd missed him at the game. C.B. was genuinely moved.

Small celebrations mean a lot to C.B. He strives to make the most out of his new life, and to give it meaning—to make it matter. And while he might use words like "miracle" and "blessing" to describe his mere survival as well as his come back, he might not describe himself as a particularly religious man. His speech teacher, Abrams, believes he is still trying to figure out the spiritual part of it.

"He'll tell you that he was mad at God for a while, and that he has this strong church family, to whom he is extremely grateful," Abrams says. "The idea that all of those people prayed for him definitely moves him, and he seems to feel that it played a part in the miracle… but he uses little religious and spiritual rhetoric. At times, he is a bit irreverent, even profane, but he never questions the power of prayer or that God is behind his own comeback. He sees it as a kind of miracle, but it just kind of stops there."

Even if C.B. doesn't talk much about the details of his spiritual and religious beliefs, he does regard his accident and subsequent survival as a miracle. And he does occasionally talk about God.

C.B. engages in a bad habit that presents health issues, possibly even shortens his lifespan—he smokes. He is fully cognizant of the risks but does it anyway. Sometimes his family and friends will ask him why he continues to smoke when he knows it might compromise his second chance at life. He's not sure why. Because he survived a tragic accident, maybe he thinks it is not in his hands. "If God wants me, he can take me," he has said. "God's not ready for me to pass on… Or maybe it's the devil. It's probably the devil…" he says with that signature twinkle in his eye. When he makes a joke, sometimes it is his way of changing the subject. Whether he wishes to avoid talking about smoking or God is unclear. Perhaps it's both.

C.B. does not remember being close to death. He does not remember whatever personal struggle he might have had, to survive those early, critical days and weeks following the fall. He was in a deep sleep, and he came out of it alive. He came out of it a changed person.

Memories of life before the fall are complete and rich and vibrant. He looks fondly on those days of actively playing sports and going to school in pursuit of his dream of becoming a teacher. Yet there are aspects of his former self that he doesn't like very much.

"I didn't care. I didn't really have goals. Even when I was at Wilkes I didn't push myself," C.B. says, thinking about his previous life. He was only 21 at the time of the accident and was still coming of age. His first attempt at college was a failure, and he was trying to make a new start at Wilkes. Then his life changed in an instant.

No one can say what he'd have made of that fresh start if he hadn't suffered a traumatic brain injury. And life with TBI presents more challenges than benefits, at least by most standards. Yet C.B. is adamant that he never gets depressed. He genuinely feels that a lot of people are worse off than he is.

C.B. has a childhood friend who was diagnosed as schizophrenic while at college. He went from a young man with a productive life and a promising future to a guy who couldn't get a job and had to rely on medication to make it through each day. C.B. has become his companion, making it a point to get his friend out in public and interacting with others as much as possible. "When he starts losing it, I calm him down," C.B. says of the role he thinks he tries to play in his friend's life. "Everybody has to have somebody there for you because…" C.B. takes a long pause, seemingly searching for the right words to express his thoughts "… Well, because I've always had someone there for me."

Fortunate for C.B., there have been many "someones" there for him throughout his long and sometimes complicated journey of survival. His comeback continues even today, and positivity still abounds among the Millers. Even though C.B.'s family is full of realists and pragmatics, they are all positive thinkers as well. They see C.B. making progress all the time. It might not be the dramatic, day-to-day and week-to-week progress they experienced, first in the hospital and in the rehab that ensued, but they see C.B. approaching his true goal—independence.

Reaching this goal has not been easy. The path here has been both tragic and triumphant, exhausting and exhilarating, depressing and uplifting—and sometimes all of those at once. But above all, it has been inspiring. Even if he did have immense support from family and friends, it was C.B. who set his own course, took it one day at a time, and had the tenacity to see it through. Tenacity combined with joy. "I hope you never get hurt," C.B. says while commenting on what he thinks has helped him come this far. "...but if you do get hurt, I hope that you'll smile. I hope that you'll always find a reason to smile."

EPILOGUE

In July 1994, Christopher B. Miller was a 21-year-old young man trying to discover his way in life. Known by his friends as "C.B.", he was giving college a second try after having had a negative experience the first time around right after high school. Playing football for a Division III private college, he was in the best physical shape of his life and looking forward to the beginning of his junior year. Suddenly and dramatically, his life changed forever.

On a hot night after a shift at his summer job, C.B. was hanging out with friends at their apartment. He ventured out onto the balcony to chat and get some fresh air. Settling into the conversation, he leaned against the porch railing. Without notice, the railing broke, and C.B. fell approximately 40 feet, landing on a concrete slab in the alleyway below.

As a result of the fall, C.B. suffered a broken wrist, bruised kidney and, most importantly, a severe traumatic brain injury. His skull was broken into almost equal-sized thirds, and the left side of his face was crushed. C.B. was rushed to a local hospital, where he spent over a month in a coma and another six weeks in intensive care. From the hospital, he went to an acute care rehabilitation center where he spent four more months receiving intensive in-patient therapy. And after release from his in-patient care, C.B. spent nearly a year engaged in outpatient therapies.

This is the story of C.B.—a story of how C.B. used his determination and iron will, combined with a keen sense of humor, to overcome challenges that have bested others. He endured several surgeries and painful therapies. He had to re-learn how to dress, bathe, eat, brush his teeth and more. All of what's referred to as "activities of daily living"—activities most of us take for granted once we've mastered them in childhood—C.B. had to learn them all over again. What's more, he had to learn how to talk and how to process and absorb new information.

Today, C.B. is a happy, educated, middle-aged man who enjoys life to the fullest. He has embraced the challenges presented to him along his journey of recovery. Currently he is developing his skills in photography, and he is dedicated to the idea of sharing his story with others so that they can be encouraged to continue to work on whatever challenges them. He wants everyone to know that if he can do it, everybody can.

ABOUT THE AUTHOR

Wes Skillings has been writing and editing the words of others for his entire professional life. As an editor, reporter and columnist for Pennsylvania newspapers with a career spanning almost four decades, he wrote human-interest stories for thousands of readers on a weekly basis. Wes lives in Wyalusing, Pennsylvania with his wife, Mary.